20 in '21
and the
YT Too

DENNY GIBSON

Copyright © 2022 Denny Gibson
Trip Mouse Publishing

All rights reserved.

ISBN: 979-8422405411

ACKNOWLEDGMENTS

I'll start where it all began by thanking John and Alice Ridge for initially making me aware of the Yellowstone Trail nearly twenty years ago. Of course, they also get my thanks for providing maps, advice, encouragement, and coffee. Thanks go to Bryan Farr for the book that made Historic US Route 20 look so inviting and got me to realize how good a partner it made for the Yellowstone Trail. His maps, advice, and encouragement are also much appreciated. The Ridges and Bryan all deserve everyone's thanks for creating and maintaining associations that promote their specific highways along with historic highways in general. I highly recommend visiting http://www.yellowstonetrail.org and https://www.historicus20.com. Thanks also to Steve Rider for his hospitality and recommendations. I very much appreciate David Habura's road and weather advice in the state of Washington as well as the coffee and muffin. Thanks to Carol Ruth, Cece Otto, Don Hatch, Perry Huntoon, and Cort Stevens for connecting with me and for finding cool places to do it. When I asked an aunt for help in fact-checking some family history for my most recent travelogue, I got a real bonus. She contributed greatly to the proofing of that book and handled the bulk of the proofreading of this one. Big thanks to my Aunt Phyllis Thomas for catching my many goofs.

Contents

1.   Plan A Goes Awry

Some may have guessed that this book's title is not as originally planned. The trip described herein was to have taken place a year earlier and provided a slightly more catchy title. I'd been hoping to drive the Yellowstone Trail for many years and in 2019 realized that combining it with a drive of US 20 would be a near-perfect two-way cross-continent road trip. The route was nearly plotted and the schedule was firming up when COVID hit. "20 in '20 and the YT Too" was not to be.

My first knowledge of the Yellowstone Trail came from an article in the very first issue of *American Road* magazine in 2003. The article was written by John and Alice Ridge who would author the magazine's "On the Yellowstone Trail" column for the next eight years. As soon as I read that first article, I knew I wanted to drive the Trail someday, and added it to the "Just Seeds" list on my website a few months later. The original Yellowstone Trail Association was formed in 1912. The Ridges were instrumental in forming the modern YTA in 1999. I joined in 2010.

Although the Yellowstone Trail began as a regional route in South Dakota, it soon grew into a coast-to-coast auto trail. Being near the northern edge of the U.S., the coasts it connected were rather far apart. Wikipedia claims the Trail's length is 3719 miles. The Ridges call it "about 3600" miles. The route that I plotted and generally followed was 3494 miles long. Two YT routes existed between Spokane and Cle Elum, Washington. I followed the north route through

Coulee City. Had I instead picked the southern route, my total would have been 3645. My plots with both routes included totaled 3864 miles. Whichever number is chosen, one thing is clear: Driving what the Yellowstone Trail Association called "A good road from Plymouth Rock to Puget Sound" requires considerable time. That requirement is the biggest reason it sat on the "Just Seeds" list so long.

I was aware of the other highway in the title, US 20, long before I became aware of the Yellowstone Trail. At 3,365 miles it is currently the longest of the U.S. Numbered Highways but that wasn't always true. When the federally controlled system of numbered highways supplanted the informal system of named auto trails in 1926, US 20 ended at the east edge of Yellowstone National Park. It was extended westward in 1940 then took over the top spot in length in 1964 when US 6 was truncated at Bishop, California.

The Yellowstone Trail was the longest of the point-to-point named auto trails in the country. The Dixie Highway included more miles of roadway but it was a network of roads connecting multiple end points. The YT connects Plymouth, Massachusetts, with Seattle, Washington. US 20 connects Boston, Massachusetts, with Newport, Oregon. Plymouth and Boston are about 35 miles apart; Seattle and Newport about 225. Looking back it's hard to believe that I didn't immediately connect these two routes, but it is a fact that I first started thinking seriously of driving US 20 on a summer morning in 2019 when I sat down to breakfast and opened my newly acquired copy of Bryan Farr's *Historic US Route 20: A Journey Across America's Longest Highway*.

The book contains a couple hundred color photographs and just about every one of them was of something I wanted to see. It slowly sunk in that this road was the perfect companion to the Yellowstone Trail. It would get me to the

Yellowstone Trail's end points while keeping me off of interstates and out of airports and promised to make getting to and from those end points just as interesting as driving between them.

The book had been published in 2015 and why it took me so long to purchase it is as much a mystery as why I only now thought of combining US 20 and the Yellowstone Trail in a major coast-to-coast road trip. Of course, it would be more than coast-to-coast. Coast-to-coast-to-coast would be more like it. Twice I've driven from one corner of Ohio to the opposite corner and back and referred to those as C2C2C, corner-to-corner-to-corner, trips. I live very close to one of those corners so starting a trip there is quite natural. I do not live on either coast.

I briefly considered using expressways to "leap" to the nearest coast before moving to a historic route but very quickly decided against it. A straight line from my home to the Atlantic coast (the nearest of the two) is over 500 miles long. A straight line from home to the eastern terminus of either US 20 or the Yellowstone Trail is over 700 miles long. A surface route would, of course, be significantly longer plus I would have to "leap back" from any place I "leaped to". I decided that was simply too much wasted motion and that the start and end of this journey would be in Ohio. At some point I started occasionally referring to it as a C2C2C2C, center-to-coast-to-coast-to-center, trip.

With that in mind, maybe the photos that make up this book's front cover make sense. They are of the four termini that define this trip arranged in the order I reached them. The first is the giant Citco sign near the eastern end of US 20 which I headed for after picking up the route in Ohio. Next is Plymouth Rock at the eastern end of the Yellowstone Trail. The third is Pioneer Park where the Yellowstone Trail ends in

Seattle and the last is the western terminus of US 20 in Newport, Oregon.

I don't know that there had ever been a US 20 association in the past, but Bryan had founded a Historic US Route 20 Association in 2012. The "historic" in the title is important. The association is not promoting the current alignment of US 20. Much of that is now divided-4-lane filled with impatient commuters and hurried vacationers. Maps of earlier historic alignments are provided on the association's website.

Winter is a good time for planning trips and plotting routes. As the winter of 2019-2020 progressed, so did the plotting for this trip. Using mostly online maps at the two associations' websites, I had the path pretty well laid out by mid-January and was starting to think about scheduling. It had not really registered with me but the USA's first COVID-19 case had been identified in Washington state on January 19, 2020. Ohio's first cases appeared on February 3. On February 18, I publicly suggested that the trip would likely happen in August. Two weeks later, spectators were banned from a sporting event in Columbus, and all Ohio bars and restaurants were closed on March 15. The primary election scheduled for March 17 was postponed, and a stay-at-home order issued on the 22nd.

With exceptions, what happened in Ohio is essentially what happened in every other state and every other country. That defines a pandemic, and the World Health Organization had declared this to be one on March 11, 2020.

> The best laid schemes o' mice an' men
> Gang aft a-gley
> – Robert Burns, 1785

2.   Plan B

Having a pandemic disrupt my travel plans was an inconvenience. Many millions have had their lives disrupted; and more than six million have had their lives ended. I will be noting the impact that COVID-19 had on my travels, but I will never ever complain about it.

With the development of vaccines and the coming of spring 2021, some restrictions related to COVID were being lifted and there was a sense that its danger really was lessening. The number of new cases began declining in January. In May it seemed reasonable to think of traveling in the near future, and so I did. Many others had already thought about it and were acting on their thoughts.

The number of people traveling in the summer of 2021 was not at pre-pandemic levels but it was much higher than it had been the summer before. Indoor spaces were deemed riskier than open areas so a lot of those traveling were heading to outdoor attractions. As a result, some national parks were limiting entry to those with advance reservations. Air travel was reviving a little but lagged automobile travel by a bunch. Traveling in a car surrounded by only your family seemed much safer then spending time in an aircraft with a couple hundred fellow passengers. When demand had suddenly plummeted in 2020, some car rental companies had stayed afloat by selling off part of their fleets which naturally caused shortages in some areas as renters started returning.

Rental car shortages did not affect me directly. Cars took up road space regardless of whether they were owned or rented. More importantly, from my point of view, most of the people in those cars were looking for places to sleep at the end of the day and so was I. I would encounter full motels several times during this trip.

My May thinking indicated a departure in early June would work. I waffled a bit on an exact date but finally picked one. The sun had been up a little less than an hour when I hit the road on June 6, 2021. I live in the southwest corner of Ohio and US 20 runs across the state at its northern edge. I had more than 160 miles to cover before the real trip actually started, and left home when I did to make sure I covered at least some of my plotted route before the day ended.

Approaching US 20 on US 127 near Alverton, OH

US 127 runs north and south through the entire state of Ohio near its western border. I picked it up about a dozen miles from home and followed it north. After a stop for breakfast, I made that big right turn and headed east just a few ticks past high noon.

3.   From the Center

I was excited to finally begin this delayed road trip but, as you might expect, not particularly excited about the area I was passing through. It is actually some rather nice looking country but it's not terribly scenic, plus I'd seen it all before.

Hal's Garage in Fayette, OH

Seeing it all before does not automatically result in remembering it all. Just a few miles after turning onto US 20, Hal's Garage, which I did not remember, caught my eye. It may have been the truck that I first noticed, but it was the creative reuse of hoods and trunk lids that prompted me to stop.

Bikes and a Buick on US 20 in Ohio

I had half halfheartedly been watching for an isolated US 20 sign to photograph to show where I was. When I came upon a pair of motorcycles, I decided to forget the idea of an isolated sign and try to catch the bikes and a sign together. Just short of Sylvania, Ohio, I got my chance. Later, when I was able to look at the picture, I discovered a bonus. Not only did I get the sign and the motorcycles, I caught a classic 1961 Buick going the opposite direction.

Historic Route 20 sign near Bellevue, OH

I confess that I was hoping for a Historic Route 20 sign when I snapped the shot of the currently official one. The motorcycles and classic car made that photo more than acceptable, but I did not completely abandon my hopes of spotting a marker for the historic route. I would be well beyond Toledo and approaching Bellevue before I saw one. I'm not saying this is the first one I passed; only the first one I saw. They are definitely not the same thing.

Seeing the Historic Route 20 sign was reassuring but not necessary. As I wrote earlier, I had plotted my intended path using online maps for the historic routes. It was loaded into my GPS and is what I would be following without depending on physical signage. The organizations promoting both Historic Route 20 and the Yellowstone Trail support signing efforts but the actual signing projects are largely local in nature. Ohio's signage on neither route is particularly good.

Of course, the current official alignment of US 20 is signed by the various highway departments it passes through.

I would be passing an awful lot of those black and white signs as I drove portions of the old route that were still being used by the current alignment. The fun of driving historic routes kicks in where route improvements have bypassed, but not destroyed, older sections. The first such older alignments I encountered on this trip were at Monroeville, Ohio.

Bypassed brick US 20 in Monroeville, OH

At Monroeville's northwest corner, a bypassed half-mile-long section is paved in asphalt. At the town's southeast corner, a section now called Norwalk Street, retains its original brick paving.

US 6, US 20, and Lake Erie west of Cleveland, OH

Things get tight where Ohio presses up against Lake Erie. Here, on the west side of Cleveland, US 20 shares pavement with US 6, the US route it replaced as longest.

1918 Veterans Memorial Bridge, Cleveland, OH

Cleveland would be the first of several large cities I would be forced to drive through. I say forced because I don't care much at all for cities and their congested traffic, but historic highways tend to go right through their centers. In Cleveland, I briefly left US 20 to take a picture of the Veterans Memorial Bridge after I'd crossed it. When it opened in 1918, it was the world's largest steel and reinforced concrete structure.

In addition to the route, I had placed several points of interest in the GPS. One of these was in the town of Painesville about halfway between Cleveland and the Pennsylvania border.

Rider's Inn with empty sign post, Painesville, OH

I had two reasons for including Rider's Inn but both were misses. One reason was that, as a B & B and restaurant, it was a possible stopping point for a meal or an overnight. It was operating on a reduced schedule and timing never clicked for either eating or sleeping. The second reason for seeking out the inn was that it was here that the first Historic Route 20 sign had been erected in May of 2014.

I planned to take a picture of the sign and drove around the block unsuccessfully looking for it. I eventually figured out that the empty post near the left edge of the picture above had been its home. Apparently, some vandals had made off with the sign. I've never understood the thinking of "fans" of historic roads who delight in making it harder for other fans (the kind without quotation marks) to enjoy a road.

Bypassed US 20 near East Springfield, PA

From Painesville, it wasn't long before I was in, and almost as quickly out of, Pennsylvania. The Keystone State contains just 45 miles of US 20 but that includes four segments of older roadway bypassed by the current alignment. All are asphalt covered and reasonably well maintained. The first is near East Springfield and the last is almost at the state line.

Bypassed US 20 at PA-NY line

Just past the State Line Methodist Church, the old alignment joins the current alignment and enters the state of New York less than a hundred yards later.

4.   To a Coast

I spent a night near Westfield, New York, and in the morning had breakfast at a place where I'd eaten before and where I would eat again before this trip was over

Main Diner, Westfield, NY

There was some luck involved in my stop at the Main Diner. Like many restaurants, it had shut down completely in the early days of the pandemic. It reopened, on weekends only, after a few months. Days were slowly added to the schedule until, not long before my visit, it was once again a seven days a week operation. I was there on a Tuesday which had been the last day added. It was, in fact, just the third Tuesday that the diner had been open in more than a year.

Marmaduke and creator Brad Anderson, Portland, NY

A few miles beyond Westfield, I passed, then turned around to photograph, a dog. It wasn't just any dog. It was Marmaduke, the popular cartoon star, and Brad Anderson, the man who drew him, in bronze. Anderson was born in Portland, where the statue is located, in 1924. The statue was unveiled in 2015.

As it did in Ohio and Pennsylvania, US 20 parallels the shore of Lake Erie in New York. The current alignment is almost always more than a mile from the lake and rather straight when compared to the bends of the shoreline. Even though you know the lake is there, it is not usually visible from the road. Then, near Irving, an older alignment now called Lake Shore Road can be reached, which does follow the shoreline closely.

Lake Erie Beach Park on Lake Shore Road, NY

A small park at the town of Lake Erie Beach offers a peaceful place to stop with a wide open view of the lake.

US 20A near Varysburg, NY

Lake Shore Road eventually becomes NY 5. At Big Tree, Historic Route 20 heads inland to join the current US 20 but

US 20A splits off almost immediately. Apparently 20A is the original route and it is the one I stayed with. I don't know whether or not it is *more* scenic than US 20 but I do know it is definitely scenic.

National Hotel, Leicester, NY

US 20A passes through Leicester which is home to the historic National Hotel. Built in 1837 and once an active station on the Underground Railroad, it operates today as a restaurant and tavern. It's another place I had identified as a possible stop that did not work out. It was open for dinner only and only on Thursday, Friday, and Saturday. I needed lunch on a Tuesday.

Mac's Drive-In, Waterloo, NY

I had better luck at Mac's Drive-In. Of course I had a bigger window to hit. My replacement for the fine dining I missed out on at the National Hotel was a fish sandwich and draft Richardson root beer hung on my door by a carhop in a tartan skirt. Mac is, after all, short for MacDougal. The place has been there since 1961 and seems to be doing quite well.

At Auburn, New York, I got a hint of the filled motels that would become something of an issue later in the trip. I found a quite satisfactory motel but it took three calls to arrange it and a little backtracking to reach it. My most recent trip of any length had been to Florida in November. COVID-19 had been much more of a concern then, and motels were anything but crowded. There were a couple of nights where I'm pretty sure I was the only one sleeping in motels with 50+ rooms. That wasn't going to happen on this trip.

Auburn Diner, Auburn, NY

Auburn has two classic diners on or near US 20. The Auburn Diner, where I had breakfast, is a 1930s Bixler about a half mile off of the route.

Hunter Dinerant, Auburn, NY

The Hunter Dinerant, which I had to skip because my belly was full, is a 1951 O'Mahony sitting right on US 20 in front of a wall full of ghost signs.

Among the things that make me chuckle are encountering a "rough road" sign after trying to dodge bone-jarring ruts for a few miles or a "scenic route" sign after being surrounded by scads of natural beauty for several minutes or longer. That happened when I passed through Lafayette, New York, and spotted the "begin" sign for the Route 20 Scenic Byway. The other end of the 108 mile long byway is in Duanesburg. I felt like I'd already been driving through some rather scenic territory but I prepared myself to have it cranked up a notch.

Scenic and Historic signs together near Bridgewater, NY

Historic routes frequently are also scenic and vise versa but they don't often brag about it. Near the midpoint of the Route 20 Scenic Byway, about a mile and a half east of Bridgewater, these two non-government routes do just that.

US 20 west of Richfield Springs, NY

The Scenic Byway does live up to the name as shown in this photo taken about eight miles beyond the sign and a few miles short of Richfield Springs.

The Tepee, Cherry Valley, NY

The Tepee has been selling souvenirs to Route 20 travelers since 1950. This was the second time I've driven by the area icon and the second time I've failed to stop. This time I failed to include the tepee's point in the picture. Those are both failures I need to correct.

American Hotel, Sharon Springs, NY

Built in 1847, the American Hotel was the first building in what is now the Sharon Springs Historic District to be placed on the National Registry of Historic Places. More than 150 buildings are included in the district.

It's big and white, just like the National Hotel pictured earlier, but those are not the only similarities. Both offer overnight accommodations and fine dining. For both, that fine dining is dinner only which leads to the similarity of me arriving at the wrong time. As this is being written, I've learned that the American Hotel became a bed and breakfast without a public restaurant at the end of 2021.

I didn't actually notice it at the time, but I must have reached the eastern end of the Route 20 Scenic Byway about

25 miles after passing Sharon Springs. The eastern end of the state of New York, which I did notice, came about 75 miles later.

Direction marker, Lenox, MA

The town of Lenox, Massachusetts, is only a half dozen miles from the state line but it takes a full dozen miles of US 20 to reach it. A stone pillar in the center of town shows the direction, but not the distance, to cities such as Albany, New York, and Stockbridge, Massachusetts. A vertical sundial is inscribed on one of the upper faces and there is evidence that a pointer was once attached. Once upon a time, this pillar may have been the town clock.

Just a few miles from Lenox, the town of Lee marks the western end of the 35-mile-long Jacob's Ladder Trail Scenic Byway. The other end is in Russel; in between is Morey Hill. In the nineteenth century, a section of the Becket Turnpike that crossed the mountain earned the name Jacob's Ladder because of its washboard like appearance and grades as steep as 22%. When the century turned and automobiles began to appear, they found this road nearly impassible. In 1910, this section was bypassed by a road with a maximum grade of 7%. Though almost flat by comparison, the new road took on the name of the abandoned road.

Jacob's Ladder Cairn, Morey Hill, MA

The road has been called "the first auto road over a mountain range" and it certainly was popular with motorists. A crowd of hundreds (some say thousands) showed up to celebrate its completion, and many brought rocks with them. A slab of local stone had been placed at the summit to commemorate the occasion and the attendees piled their rocks around it. Over the years, the cairn has been moved, reorganized, and mortared but it is still there beside the road.

Bryan Farr, Founder of Historic Route 20 Association

The town of Chester, Massachusetts, is well beyond the actual "ladder" section but it is part of the Jacob's Ladder Trail Scenic Byway. Chester is where I connected with Historic US Route 20 Association founder, Bryan Farr. The association shares a building that was once a Ford dealership with Carm's Restaurant where we had breakfast and jabbered about old roads. The food and conversation were both great. I'd had several online conversations with Bryan as I planned this trip, but this was our first in person meeting. We would do it again before the trip was over.

Wayside Inn, Sudbury, MA

When I left Bryan, my plan was to spend the night at Longfellow's Wayside Inn if a room was available. Due to bad comprehension, bad math, or both, I had it in my head that I could not possibly get through Boston by the end of the day. I intended to stop just short of the city then dash through in the morning.

For better or worse, I realized my mistake before I booked a room or even asked. That means I have no idea whether it was fully booked or not but I now think it likely was. The Wayside Inn's story goes all the way back to 1716, and it had long been on my list of places to visit. I took pictures while walking about with a Wayside Inn Draft in my hand.

Boston and New York City have me buffaloed like no others. I don't exactly like driving in any city but not even Los Angeles, in which I *really* dislike driving, makes me as anxious as these two. I've driven in both of them without any real problems, and don't think I'm actually afraid of them. I don't expect to get in a big wreck, but I do expect to get lost or involved in some sort of tense situation. I'm sure that having that attitude contributes to it happening. On this visit to Boston, I almost got to my destination — but not quite.

Kenmore Square, Boston, MA

My destination was right next to that Citco sign where a big green sign states that Newport, Oregon, is 3,365 miles away on US 20. I had encountered construction, absent or unreadable street signs, wrong turns, and missed turns. There was nothing that I hadn't encountered in almost every city I'd ever been in as well as a fair number of small towns, but it all served to reinforce my dread of Boston. Even though the street looks almost empty in the photo above, it was here that I surrendered. I snapped the picture just after the cars ahead of me dashed through the light at the next intersection, and just before the cars next to me got the signal to dash to it. I was, once again, through some not quite understood goof of my own, in a left turn lane.

I'm sure that most Bostonians and some Cincinnatians would have at least tried jumping ahead of the pack. I might have too if I'd known for sure that the sign was at the very next intersection. But I didn't. I turned left, and before I did I decided that I'd had enough, and was not going to crawl around another block. I hit the "out" button on the GPS.

Plymouth Harbor, Plymouth, MA

I headed to Plymouth, and a motel, and dinner by the bay. I missed the very end of US 20 by a block but I'd made it to the coast. I can live with that.

5.   From a Coast

The first step in traveling C2C2C2C was complete. I had made it from the center to the first coast and was now in Plymouth, Massachusetts, ready to switch directions and highways. In the real world, these two things must be done separately.

Plymouth Rock and Mayflower II, Plymouth, MA

The eastern terminus of the Yellowstone Trail, as shown on the Yellowstone Trail Association map, is on North Street where it meets Water Street less than fifty yards from Plymouth Rock. North Street is currently one-way eastbound for all of its 500 feet. So I drove that bit eastward to the terminus then circled around to its other end at Court Street to begin my westward journey on the Yellowstone Trail.

High Street, Duxbury, MA

A construction detour was encountered almost immediately but it was a short one. I was soon out of Plymouth and into some rather quiet Massachusetts countryside.

Newton Street, Weston, MA

Three hours later, I was in very similar surroundings on the west side of Boston. Like US 20 and virtually every other pre-Interstate Highway System route, the Yellowstone Trail passed right through most cities. I encountered more construction and missed another turn or two, but I'd made it through Boston going both east and west and was now done with it for this trip.

East of Indiana, the Yellowstone Trail has largely been replaced by US 20. Not all of the named auto trail was incorporated into the numbered U.S. highway but much of it was. East of Springfield, Massachusetts, this was almost totally the case. That means I was seeing the same things driving west that I had seen going east.

Historic Route 20 Visitor Center, Chester, MA

That included the building in Chester where I had met Bryan Farr the day before. It was now late afternoon, and the restaurant and visitor center were closed. I took advantage of the absence of parked cars to snap a picture of the former gas station and one time Ford dealership they occupy.

The fact that I was sort of retracing my steps made the rain I encountered when I reentered New York not much of a concern at all. It was never particularly heavy, and, although the streets were wet, it had pretty much stopped by the time I reached Albany.

New York Capitol, Albany, NY

With memories of Boston fresh in my mind, Albany seemed quite mild. The Yellowstone Trail actually passed behind New York's capitol but missing a turn by a block put me right in front of it.

Steve Rider, friend, road fan, and memorabilia collector extraordinaire lives in Albany. He lives, in fact, not much more than a hundred yards from US 20. It would have made sense to visit Steve while eastbound but that didn't quite work out so I slipped over from the Yellowstone Trail while headed west. Only about two miles separates the two routes at this point.

Steve Rider, memorabilia collector, Albany, NY

I'd been here once before, about six years ago, but there were plenty of new things in his garage/museum along with things I had overlooked on the first visit. Plus, it was great just to catch up with Steve.

Old Fort Johnson, Fort Johnson, NY

Old Fort Johnson is right on the Yellowstone Trail some thirty miles northwest of Albany. Built around 1749, it's a place I was not aware of until Steve suggested it. There is a museum inside but the site would not open for the season until about a week after my stop.

Stanley Theater, Utica, NY

In 1928, the Stanley Theater in Utica was opening just as the original Yellowstone Trail Association was closing. The theater has been completely restored and hosts a variety of events including Utica Symphony Orchestra performances.

West of Utica, my itinerary began to be affected by that full motel situation I hinted at earlier combined with arranging a first meeting with a long time friend.

Today, most of us likely have at least a few online "friends" that we have never met in the real world. This friendship, however, originated in those pre-Facebook days when email groups supported by Yahoo! and others were the closest thing we had to social media. It was 2004 when Carol Ruth responded to my egroup call for suggestions on a trip in Pennsylvania. We've since communicated several times but, had never met during the seventeen years that followed. When she realized, from my online journal, that I was going to be in her extended neighborhood, she contacted me about a meeting. Knowing the area and my penchant for breweries, she suggested a brewery in Canandaigua and even mentioned a motel she thought I'd like. I anticipated a night spent somewhere around Syracuse with a leisurely drive the next day followed by a few brews and a night in Canandaigua.

That might have worked had I started my hunt on the east side of Syracuse but that seemed too early and I decided I should get beyond the city before stopping. When I pulled into a parking lot and started making calls, I discovered that motels in front of me that looked promising were already filled. As my hunt reached nearer and nearer to Canandaigua, I decided to call the motel Carol had suggested to see if a room was available that night. The answer was yes, so I ended up flipping my motel and brewery plans.

Miami Motel, Canandaigua, NY

The motel was a real winner. Built in 1952 and restored by the current owners over nineteen years, it offers a bit of Miami, Florida, in the Finger Lakes region of New York.

With Carol Ruth at Naked Dove Brewing, Canandaigua, NY

Because I had scurried to Canandaigua rather than dawdling as planned, I found myself with time to do laundry before the brewery, which was essentially next door to the motel, opened and Carol arrived. She brought along some Yellowstone Trail information for me to take with me and a binder of photos to look through as we sampled craft beer. Even though I've become rather familiar with the phenomenon, I'm still impressed with how easily road fans slip into conversation. As soon as we've said hello, we're off comparing notes about roads we've both driven or asking questions and sharing stories about roads that only one has experienced. That instant conversation is not, I know, unique to us with an interest in old roads but something likely to happen with any meeting of folks with a common interest. It's a wonderful thing.

Buffalo Well Products, Akron, NY

Could starting from a brewery next to a beach themed motel have anything to do with me finding mostly whimsical camera subjects for my remaining time in New York state? The first was a yard full of welder's art in Akron.

Welcome to Farnham, NY

In Buffalo, a poorly designed, or possibly just poorly comprehended detour, had me scrambling to get across the river and out of town. I don't recall being very much bothered by that, but even if it did tone down my smile a little, it was back to a full grin when I spotted the Hollywood-like sign on a railroad embankment in Farnham with its population of 368.

Partially due to what I perceive as a motel desert in western New York, my last night in in the state was spent at the same place (Theater Motel) as my first and I had dinner at the same place (Calarco's) too. I also had breakfast at the same place but that was no accident.

Main Diner, Westfield, NY

I really like Westfield's Main Diner. Since I included an exterior view on my eastbound stop, I'll use a shot of the briefly empty counter this time.

Grace Bedell meets Abraham Lincoln, Westfield, NY

I hope history teachers never quit telling the story about Lincoln growing a beard during his presidential campaign in response to a letter from twelve year old Grace Bedell. Grace lived in Westfield. The two met on February 16, 1861, when Abe visited Westfield. This park and statue were dedicated in 1999. I took the picture one score and two years later.

I took even less pictures in Pennsylvania westbound than I did eastbound as it was raining for the entire distance. It finally let up somewhere west of Painesville and had completely stopped by the time I drove through a surprisingly uncongested Cleveland.

Erie Lake near Lorain, OH

About halfway across Ohio, the road is quite close to the shore of Lake Erie which was looking its summertime best as I drove by. At Toledo the route begins angling southward in order to reach Fort Wayne, Indiana.

Carter's Produce Stand near Wauseon, OH

As the space between towns increases, the width of the roads connecting them usually decreases. Two-lane roads definitely pass more produce stands than the big interstates do. Where a farmer is selling some extra produce from his own fields, the stand might be just a couple of boards or an old beat up table. But some are a lot more elaborate and support a real commercial enterprise..

I crossed US 127 about sixteen miles west of the big wooden ear of corn. That's the road I followed north from home to begin this adventure. Its intersection with US 20, where I turned east nine days earlier, is about ten miles to the north. Indiana is less than twenty miles away.

6.   Again From the Center

We all know that western Ohio is not very near the center of a coast-to-coast drive. When the endpoints of that drive are Plymouth Rock and Puget Sound, the center is probably somewhere around the eastern edge of South Dakota. But western Ohio is where I picked up US 20 to start this trip and where I'll eventually return to end it. I'm using it as a dividing line for trip segments and I'm calling it center because that starts with a 'c'. I will not allow details of geography and distance get in the way of driving C2C2C2C.

I mentioned that the Yellowstone Trail starts angling southwest around Toledo but it really gets serious about it near my "center" at US 127. It now heads directly toward Fort Wayne and the most southerly point of the entire Trail. From there, it turns toward Indiana's northwest corner where it will hug Lake Michigan through Illinois and into Wisconsin.

Old Trail Road west of Columbia City, IN

The Yellowstone Trail leaves Fort Wayne on Leesburg Road then the name changes to Old Trail Road at the Whitley County line. Signs do not specify any particular old trail but we know.

Retired gas station, Plymouth, IN

I've spent very little time in Plymouth, Indiana, even though I have passed through it several times. Before this pass on the Yellowstone Trail, I've visited multiple times on the Dixie Highway and Lincoln Highway, and I've visited at least once on the Michigan Road which predates not only the named auto trails but the autos that begat them.

Modern Yellowstone Trail sign west of Plymouth, IN

About a half dozen miles beyond Plymouth I spotted something that might seem extremely mundane but which I consider a highlight of the trip. A Yellowstone Trail sign stood in someone's front yard several feet from the road. I'm guessing that the setback was to keep it on private property and not in violation of any law. What made this so exciting was that it was the first time I had seen one of these signs "in the wild".

I mentioned earlier that signage for historic highways is generally the responsibility of local organizations and can vary wildly. The area around Plymouth has a very active Yellowstone Trail group so I should have expected some nearby portions of the route to be marked. The sign in the picture is the first I spotted but I saw quite a few more as I continued driving. I noted at the time that I thought it possible to follow the Yellowstone Trail between Plymouth and Valparaiso simply by following the signs. Nice job, Plymouth and Hamlet.

Yellowstone Trail Road near Hamlet, IN

Some sections of the route in the area were well maintained gravel and one section was even officially signed as Yellowstone Trail.

Once I was past Valparaiso and approaching Chicago, there were no gravel roads and few open spaces. My route took me right through Gary, Indiana, and past a big sign pointing to the childhood home of the Jackson 5. Traffic was still fairly light so I turned at the sign for a half-mile side trip.

Jackson family home, Gary, IN

You can use the address on the sign or just look for the only house in the neighborhood with a security fence and messages from fans.

Sitting between Gary and and the state line is East Chicago, home of Indiana Harbor and Ship Canal. It is also home to multiple large clusters of railroad tracks. Train cars, semi-trucks, and Great Lake freighters abound. Construction of the harbor started in 1901 so The Yellowstone Trail had to deal with it from the beginning although I'm sure it was a much simpler task in the 1920s than it is now.

Road closure in East Chicago, IN

On the day I passed through here, the path of the Yellowstone Trail was blocked in multiple places. Some of the closures were for construction projects and were temporary. At least one looked quite permanent. Apparently, I should have bailed sooner because by the time I reached what I think was a permanent blockade, I was in a line of semis being funneled through a gate. The guy at the gate got me over to the exit lane without actually calling me an idiot and I worked my way back to a main road and on to the town of Whiting, Indiana. The path that the Yellowstone Trail followed into Illinois remains popular. It is now followed by US 12, US 20, and US 41.

Water Tower, Chicago, IL

I don't actually like driving in Chicago but it doesn't spook me like Boston. That's a good thing, I suppose, because the Yellowstone Trail runs right through the heart of Chicago and right past those lions guarding the art museum, Grant Park, and that famous Water Tower which was already forty-three years old when the original Yellowstone Trail Association was formed in 1912.

Lake Michigan near Evanston, IL

The Yellowstone Trail basically follows the Lake Michigan shore through the state of Illinois. It is an area pretty much filled by Chicago and its suburbs which could easily make the YT traveler think the state is nothing but pavement and tall buildings. Admittedly, that is mostly true but there are some beautiful lake views and green spaces north of the city.

In following the lake shore, the road north is frequently forced to the left by the water. These are natural curves with no alternatives so that driving instructions have no reason to even mention them. However, when the route subsequently turns to the right to track the water's edge, there often are alternatives and some action is required to stay on the route. For me, this meant the GPS calling for a right turn. For the most part, this section of the Yellowstone Trail follows Sheridan Road. This resulted in the GPS repeatedly telling me to "turn right on Sheridan Road" with absolutely no other instructions in between. This might be the only place in the world where you can turn right on Sheridan Road a half-dozen times in succession without driving in a circle.

Modern Yellowstone Trail Sign, Saint Francis, WI

Not surprisingly, Wisconsin is a pretty good place to find Yellowstone Trail signs. Many shared posts with official government signs indicating they were not just tolerated but embraced.

Ardy & Ed's Drive In, Oshkosh, WI

It's also a good place to find detours but that hardly makes it special. I mention them here only because it was a detour that caused me to approach Ardy & Ed's Drive In from a side road rather than on the Yellowstone Trail proper. That meant I initially missed it and had to turn around but it was certainly worth it. The drive-in opened in 1948 as an A & W Root Beer stand. In 1972, the A & W franchise was dropped and the name changed to Ardy & Ed's by owners Edward and Ardythe Timm. I don't know when the skating car hops first appeared but I know that they now appear at your car door just about instantly.

Yellowstone Trail marker in Caddott, WI

As I mentioned, there are quite a few modern Yellowstone Trail signs in Wisconsin but that's just not enough for some people. That includes the people in the town of Cadott who mark the Trail with a wheel and rock display.

Indianhead Motel, Chippewa Falls, WI

And a bland plastic motel sign isn't enough for some people including me and the owners of the Indianhead Motel in Chippewa Falls, Wisconsin. It misses being directly on the Trail by barely a hundred yards, and that gorgeous sign obviously makes it more than worth the short drive. Nice rooms and owners too.

Alice & John Ridge, Yellowstone Trail Association founders

Perhaps not everyone understood my comment about not being surprised to find Yellowstone Trail signs in Wisconsin. Wisconsin is home to Alice and John Ridge who founded the modern Yellowstone Trail Association in 1999. There is naturally significant support for both the route and the association in the state.

The Ridges live south of Chippewa Falls and agreed to a visit while I was in the area. As I've mentioned before, road fans have little trouble diving into conversation whether they have met before or not. That was definitely the case with the Ridges and I think Alice, John, and I could have easily spent the entire day talking about old roads, old trips, planned trips, and dreamed-of trips. When I at last pulled myself away to return to the road, I left with a wonderful surprise.

The Ridges have been researching and writing about the Yellowstone Trail for many years. At the time of my visit, they were just wrapping up a major work on the highway. That book, *A Good Road from Plymouth Rock to Puget Sound*, has since been published and is highly recommended. Subtitled *A Modern Guide to Driving the Historic Yellowstone Trail 1912-1930*, it is indeed a guide but is so much more. Stories and details about early automobile travel make an armchair trip almost as good as the real thing.

They had just turned over what was hoped to be the final manuscript to the printer and presented me with some of the last round of markups which were about to be discarded. I returned to my travels armed with near final versions of the chapters covering all of the route that still lay before me.

Minnesota capitol, Saint Paul, MN

That included the state of Minnesota where I rolled by the capitol in Saint Paul with no problems at all. The lack of problems did not continue through Saint Paul's twin city of Minneapolis. A number of construction related closures kept me from strictly following the Yellowstone Trail but I survived the city and was on the proper route when I left town.

Yellowstone Trail about two miles east of Stewart, MN

Stewart, MN, water tower

With a 2020 population of 535, Stewart, Minnesota, about sixty miles west of Minneapolis, is not a big town and neither is it famous. The only person listed by name in its Wikipedia entry is Dr. D. A. Stewart who plotted and named the town in 1888. But two visuals I encountered in passing through Stewart made an impression and have stuck with me. One is the parallel and arrow straight lines of the utility poles, railroad tracks, and gravel road approaching the town from the east.

The rails, now owned by the Twin Cities & Western Railroad Company, were put in place in the 1870s as part of the Hastings & Dakota Railway. The poles and road came along later and, as was common, simply followed the path established by the railroad. There are details in the photo that someone intent on proving it was not taken in 1920 could use to their advantage but the general appearance is probably pretty much as it was a century ago.

The impression made by the 1923 water tower is also partially due to the fact that it looks something like it did nearly a hundred years ago but also due to the fact that it probably looks better. Some of those 535 people are proud of their town and I'd like to think all of them are. I'm proud of having merely passed through on a sunny day in June.

Hill's Unique Gifts, Hector, MN

The value of the Ridges' markups was obvious to me as soon as I received them. Shareable proof appeared the very next day. In our morning chat, they had described an interesting store in the town of Hector. As I was about to leave the town, I realized that I had seen no such store. I turned to the pages of the not-quite-published book to see that the place I was looking for, Hill's Unique Gifts, was actually a couple of blocks off of the Yellowstone Trail as it stair-stepped through town.

Missing it would certainly have been a shame as it was exactly the "delightful tourist trap" the Ridges had said it was. Teri, the owner, is a combination clerk, guide, historian, and comedian. As the Ridges say, the place is filled with things you don't need but should not leave without.

Giant Corn Gazebo, Olivia, MN

Just a few days after photographing an ear of corn carved from a tree trunk in Ohio, I discovered a bigger ear atop a building in Olivia, the official "Corn Capital of Minnesota".

Car show in Montevideo, MN

After spending a night in Montevideo, I discovered that rain had passed through during the night and washed some of the dirt off of my car. Then I was surprised to find truly clean cars setting up for the Fiesta Days Car Show as I headed through the downtown. I can't promise you'll be as lucky.

Viking statue in Milan, MN

Anyone who has ever listened to Garrison Keillor knows that a large portion of Minnesota's settlers were Scandinavian. Small but mighty Milan was founded by Norwegians in 1879 and the town remains quite proud of their Scandinavian roots. There is evidence of that in murals and other pieces of public art including a tree-sized horned Viking.

Something that surprised me on the trip was the number of times I passed collections of old but only mostly dead automobiles lined up by the road. By "only mostly dead", I don't mean that they were capable of self powered motion but that they were salvageable with "a little touch up and a little paint; OK, make that a lot of touch up and a bunch of paint. Such sights are fairly common in the arid and rust-free southwest but are something I did not expect to see in the snowy north.

Old cars near Odessa, MN

The cars in the photograph above face US 75. I first spotted them from the Yellowstone Trail which runs behind those trees before merging with the US route. I turned onto east bound US 75 just far enough to snap a few pictures. A row of cars on the other side of that fence includes a 1960 Edsel.

The South Dakota state line is just a few miles west of those cars, and about an equal distance beyond that line is the town of Milbank.

Restored windmill, Milbank, SD

Milbank is home to a wonderfully restored windmill. It was built in 1884 by a man named Holland which seems like a very good name for a windmill builder, although this Holland was from England.

Yellowstone Trail near Waubay, SD

Waubay, South Dakota, is another place that came up over coffee with the Ridges in Wisconsin. Wetlands define the area and roadways have never been what one could call "high and dry". But rising water levels in recent years have resulted in some roads being elevated and some being closed. Both categories contain portions of the Yellowstone Trail. To the north, Waubay Lake has risen just a couple of feet this century while the much closer Bitter Lake to the south has risen something like ten feet. Of course, the rising began well before the century did.

Seagulls near Waubay, SD

The day was cloudy but dry. The wind was not particularly heavy but it was definitely a notch or two above what I would consider a light breeze. It was enough to allow seagulls to windsurf and stay right beside my car when I stopped to take a picture. Those gulls, by the way, are about 1200 miles from either coast.

Lasting impressions were recorded by my ears as well as my eyes. With the windows open, the sound of waves lapping at the road could be heard – on both sides of the car. The sound was a little unsettling when I let my mind start exploring some "what ifs". What if the wind speed doubled or tripled? What if it were raining? And the big one, what if I come back to drive this road in ten or twenty years?

Joe Parmley home, Ipswich, SD

I had been looking forward to reaching Ipswich, South Dakota, but I had not been looking hard enough. Ipswich is the "Home of the Yellowstone Trail". It's where Joe Parmley lived when he founded the Yellowstone Trail Association and where the association was initially headquartered. Parmley's home and his land office still stand and both now function as museums. Reportedly, both museums are open three days each week during the summer. I had not looked into their schedule before arriving and was there on one of the other four days.

1912-1916 YTA headquarters, Ipswich, SD

Parmley was a land agent and maintained the YTA in his office from its 1912 founding until 1916 when Hal Colley became General Manager and moved the association's headquarters twenty-five miles east to Aberdeen.

Cars near Morristown, SD

Near Morristown, South Dakota, I spotted a second display of "only mostly dead" classics in as many days. These were, for some unknown reason, predominately Pontiacs.

Eye catching sign in Lemmon, SD

I thought the scrap-based sculpture was just a great way to attract attention, but I've since learned that there's more to it than that. From the museum's website:

> *"The concept of a cowboy ridding* [sic] *a dinosaur fits in with the creation theme found through out* [sic] *the inside of the museum."*

That makes me wish I had made more of an effort to check it out.

The north edge of Lemmon, South Dakota, is tightly pressed against the North Dakota border. About a dozen miles west of town, US 12 and the Yellowstone Trail angle across that border to nip the southwest corner of the state.

Park in Hettinger, ND

Hettinger, North Dakota, is obviously proud of its place on the Yellowstone Trail. One of the pictured panels contains information about three Adams County structures that are on the National Registry of Historic Places. The other is filled with YT facts and photos and the conical stone at the back of the park is completely YT related. In places, rocks like this, called hoodoos, were often painted yellow to mark the way.

Among the pointers the Ridges had given me during our chat was one for North Dakota. They suggested that I stop at Van Horn's Western & Antique Auto Museum, but the suggestion was triggered more by the museum's owner than its contents. Unfortunately, JD VanHorn, the man responsible for everything in the museum, had gone to Montana for the day on business. Even though JD was absent, I got a sense of the man from his museum which is actually both a museum and an ice cream parlor.

Van Horn's Museum, Marmouth, ND

Cars are the main thing and there is a bunch of them. All appear well cared for and many have been restored. Almost all have placards with at least the make and model shown. Some are accessorized with mannequins. There are three buildings filled with cars, wagons, saddles, and other items. Some of the items are well organized; others not so much. The oldest cars are in the main building which you can tour for $10. For another $10, you get to tour the other two buildings and receive, when you're done, a big scoop of ice cream, a ball point pen, a postcard, and a calendar with JD's picture. I really am sorry I didn't get to meet the guy.

7.   To the Other Coast

US 12 has taken over the Yellowstone Trail's job in this area and that's what carried me for the first twenty-some miles into Montana. The current US 12 alignment departs from the Yellowstone Trail at the small town of Plevna, and that's where I departed from US 12 on what was probably the longest unpaved section of the entire trip.

Tree near Plevna, MT

Between Plevna and Fallon, the road does go through the towns of Ismay and Mildred and I cannot be certain that one or the other doesn't contain a block or so of pavement. However, I am rather confident that the forty-five miles of roadway outside of those clusters consist entirely of gravel, dirt, and the wooden deck of a single bridge.

Direction sign just north of Ismay, MT

Wooden decked bridge north of Mildred, MT

The photos I've included from this section show things it has just one of. There is a shade tree shielding a bit of road, a hand painted sign pointing to civilization, and the aforementioned bridge.

Everyone has their own idea of where the American West begins and those who place it somewhere in the Dakotas could be right. That dinosaur riding cowboy back in Lemmon, South Dakota, did look right at home. But, as I have said when traveling the more southerly Lincoln Highway, I think of it as being the east border of Wyoming. That borderline extends north to define the east edge of Montana so it makes sense for me to consider it the West's beginning when traveling through the northern tier of states. Part of my reasoning in picking Wyoming is the fact that there is no doubt about being in the west once you've reached Cheyenne. On the Yellowstone Trail, that same sort of logic applies to Miles City.

Cars at the edge of Miles City, MT

But before I reached the Wild West heart of Miles City, I paused at another collection of "only mostly dead" cars. These, like the ones at Morristown, SD, are overwhelmingly Pontiacs. I have no idea why the north has so many cars in display formations let alone why so many are Pontiacs.

Olive Hotel, Miles City, MT

The Historic Olive Hotel was my home in Miles City. The 102-year-old hotel has some rough edges but was more than satisfactory for me. Due to staffing issues, the dining room was open only for breakfast and the lounge not at all.

Montana Bar, Miles City, MT

There are several other restaurants in the area, and dealing with the lack of a hotel lounge was easy with 1908's Historic Montana Bar little more than a block away.

After breakfast in the hotel restaurant I headed out of town, but a low-tire warning light prompted a quick turnaround. I don't know if finding a gas station with free air was a miracle or just western hospitality but I sure did appreciate it. The first warning had surprised me; the second one did not. With several miles of gravel road ahead of me, I again turned around, crossed my fingers, and eased the car back to Miles City.

Tire repair, Miles City, MT

It has been my experience that flat tires are hardly ever repairable unless it's a valve stem problem. I had assumed I would be buying at least one new tire and was shocked when the folks at Tire-Rama found a screw in the tire, sealed the leak, and had me back on the road in under an hour for less than twenty dollars. The free air may or may not have been a miracle. This most certainly was.

Yellowstone Trail and Yellowstone River near Sanders, MT

My route between Miles City and Billings contained a mixture of paved and unpaved two-or-less-lane road. After reaching the Yellowstone River at Fallon, the Yellowstone Trail generally followed the river from that point on west. Sometimes it followed rather loosely, and the two might be separated by a few miles. At other points, such as the town of Sanders, they were separated by a few feet.

I was actually seeing this part of Montana for the second time in my life. I passed through here in 2016 when I was on the way home from a long trip and sticking, for the most part, to expressways. On this trip, I avoided the expressways as much as possible. Of course, even with my sights set on home on that earlier trip, exits were taken and stops made when appropriate. A stop that was repeated on this trip was at Pompey's Pillar although I didn't have to follow an exit sign this time. The Yellowstone Trail pretty much led me right to it.

Pompey's Pillar, MT

The Corps of Discovery (a.k.a. Lewis and Clark Expedition) temporarily split into two groups on July 3, 1806. The group led by Clark reached this 150 foot tall pillar on July 25.

Pompey's Pillar, MT (2016)

Clark named the giant outcropping Pompy's Tower after Sacajawea's son. The first editor of the expedition's journals changed this to Pompey's Pillar and it is sometimes written without the apostrophe. William Clark carved his name and the date on the pillar, and I'll readily admit that my attitude toward two-century-old graffiti is much different than what I feel about the modern stuff.

When I was at the pillar in 2016, it was being cleared of people due to an approaching thunder storm. I barely made it to the historic inscription but I did get a decent picture. In 2021, I had plenty of time to explore the pillar but the last few feet of the walkway at the inscription was closed for some unknown reason. The carving could be seen fairly well but one corner was obscured so I've used a photo from 2016.

About thirty miles beyond the pillar, the Yellowstone Trail goes right through the city of Billings. I spent the night in a chain motel there but did not do much exploring. I was more interested in something about thirty miles on its other side.

New Atlas Bar, Columbus, MT

Although it is a little newer than Miles City's Montana Bar, the New Atlas Bar in Columbus seems every bit as authentic. The bar opened in 1916 with the "New" getting added to the name around 1949. The preceding picture shows one of two large wooden backbars from the 1890s that were moved here from other bars when the Atlas opened.

Spittoons in New Atlas Bar, Columbus, MT

Multiple sources say that there was originally no furniture in the bar area. This was very intentional as, according to a newspaper report, the bar "will be a no loafing place, and those who want to rest will have to find accommodations in the billiards room". It seems you could spit but not sit.

A little less than ten miles west of Columbus, I turned onto a stretch of original Yellowstone Trail now signed Springtime Road. The small town of Springtime once stood here but the post office closed in 1936, and today there is really nothing left.

Yellowstone Trail near Springtime, MT

The road begins as asphalt but soon becomes reasonably well maintained gravel that continues for most of the nearly fifteen mile drive to Reed Point.

Reed Point, MT

There was once enough life in Reed Point to support two grain elevators but both have been idle for a long time. There wasn't much life in the town when I was there although it has fared much better than Springtime and still has its post office. The pandemic may be responsible for some of the closed storefronts given that some closures seemed temporary. A sign on the Waterhole Saloon promised it would reopen in July, and there is evidence online that that happened.

The Yellowstone Trail and the Yellowstone River have been traveling companions for about 300 miles when they part ways directly north of the big park that shares their name. The YT mainline never quite reached its namesake park but there was a fifty-five-mile-long spur that led from Livingston, Montana, to the Roosevelt Arch at Yellowstone National Park's north entrance. US 89 fills that role today.

Murray Hotel, Livingston, MT

I knew that the historic Murray Hotel in Livingston would be a great place to stay and actually called once I had a date in hand but was not at all surprised to find it full. That's not entirely a bad thing since the mid-summer rate would have made a noticeable bump in my budget.

Murray Hotel, Livingston, MT

My budget did, however, accommodate a look inside the lobby and a bit of refreshment in the hotel lounge.

Sacajawea Park, Livingston, MT

I did something of a walkabout in downtown Livingston then drove to Sacajawea Park before leaving town. The pictured statue shows the Shoshone guide on horseback with her son on her arm. That son was born while Sacajawea was with Lewis and Clark and given the name Jean Baptiste Charbonneau. He was then nicknamed Pomp by Clark who named that rock tower seen a few pages back after him.

I mentioned early on that a lot more people were traveling in 2021 than in 2020 and that a lot of those travelers were targeting outdoor spaces. I had felt a little of the resulting load on lodging when I passed through the Finger Lakes region of New York, and wasn't the least bit surprised when it became even more evident as I neared the granddaddy of all U.S. outdoor spaces, Yellowstone National Park. However, I had the idea that things would loosen up once I was past the gateway city of Livingston. By the end of the day, I would learn just how wrong I was but in the meantime I would blissfully enjoy some of the best scenery of the trip.

The drive through Bozeman and Three Forks was pleasant and sometimes even interesting but it became much more interesting about a half mile beyond Willow Creek where the pavement ends. This is, I believe, about where the eastern slope of Harrison Hill begins.

Yellowstone Trail near Willow Creek, MT

It's possible that the road between Willow Creek and Harrison may have been entirely gravel at one time. If so, it has been quite a while since it has been refreshed. Much of the road is now essentially bare dirt. Signs mark sections as "IMPASSABLE WHEN WET" and I believe them. This is no doubt the gumbo that the Ridges warn of when writing about Harrison Hill in their book. On this day, the road was dry and, despite some clouds in the sky, it was fairly certain it would stay that way.

Start of descent to Harrison, MT

The preceding picture was taken near the start of the descent on the hill's western slope about three miles from US 287. The following picture was taken near the start of the steepest part of the descent about a mile from US 287.

Jackson Morgan Horse Ranch near Harrison, MT

About two minutes before snapping the picture of what I later learned was a horse ranch, I had encountered a girl and her dog walking along the road. I had not yet even spotted the ranch and assumed I was many miles from civilization. I could not imagine what this young lady, whom I guessed to be about twenty years old, was doing on this empty and isolated dirt road. With a smile, she assured me that she was just fine and pointed down the road while volunteering that she was "staying in that house". I moved on a hundred yards or so then paused to take a picture of "that house".

The house is hidden in the cluster of trees and not really what prompted the picture. It was the grass lined two-track and the Tobacco Root Mountains beyond that grabbed my attention and yielded one of my favorite photographs of the trip.

I'm guessing that two-track is partly responsible for Harrison Hill's reputation. I have little doubt that it would qualify as "IMPASSABLE WHEN WET". I eased my way down the slope and past the group of buildings then on across US 287.

At the end of the day, as I worked on the trip journal, I fired up Google Maps to see if I could locate those buildings in satellite images. Even though the girl I had met on the road wasn't as far from other humans as I first thought, I wondered just how far away she was. I found the buildings and quickly determined that she was slightly less than a mile from the house when I spoke with her. A surprise and bonus was that the cluster of buildings had a name: Jackson Morgan Horse Ranch.

That led to a visit to the ranch's website and another surprise. The site's front page was a memorial to William T Jackson, the ranch's owner and Jackson family patriarch. He had died five days earlier at age 96. I don't know for certain but I've a hunch that was his granddaughter I met on the Yellowstone Trail.

The scenic surroundings continued on the other side of US 287 and the roadway became asphalt. That continued through Cardwell and Whitehall. I found gravel waiting when I turned onto what is now called Airport Lane about five miles beyond Whitehall.

Taxi advertisement in Pipestone Pass, MT

It sometimes seems like I miss more of the smaller roadside artifacts than I should so I was very happy to spot this ultimate ghost sign beside the gravel road in Pipestone Pass. I knew of the Butte Taxi advertisement but did not have an exact location so was far from certain that I would see it. Plus, it seemed possible that the painted sign had faded to the point of vanishing. It has faded some when compared to photos taken ten or more years ago but it is still quite readable and I now have some fairly close coordinates (N45° 49.145' W112° 18.338').

Seeing that taxi ad was a trip highlight, and I'm sure it helped my mood through what followed. I was about to realize that the lodging situation was not going to ease up beyond Livingston as I had naively anticipated.

Butte would have been a convenient spot to end the day, and there were some places there I would have enjoyed revisiting but it was not to be. Online searches and several phone calls came up empty. With a sense of urgency beginning to move in, I looked at a map and picked Missoula as the next city with significant motel potential. The first two motels I called were completely filled. The third reported just one room left. I took it. In hindsight, I would have been better off sleeping in my car.

Because of the distance to Missoula, I was resigned to hitting the expressway at some point but wanted to get in as much Yellowstone Trail as possible before that happened. A trick I use in situations like this is to use my GPS equipped phone to set a course to the off route target while continuing to follow the plotted route on the Garmin. The phone helps me pick the best spot to exit the planned route to reach a restaurant or motel or some other desired off route point. I occasionally glanced at the phone as I continued following the Yellowstone Trail. My goal was to get the time to the motel under an hour which I considered a reasonable amount of time to backtrack in the morning. The overriding factor was sunset. I didn't really want to be driving anywhere after dark and definitely not on some unpaved narrow road. Aside from safety considerations, I simply didn't want to miss seeing – in daylight – any of the Yellowstone Trail or its scenic surroundings.

When I reached the west side of Butte, things weren't looking too bad. The room I had reserved was about two hours away on the interstate, and I had nearly that much daylight left. Time spent on a winding historic route was not equivalent to time spent on an expressway but it seemed likely that staying the course until near sunset would get me to within an hour or less of my motel.

Roadblock, Butte, MT

Then I hit a dead end. I had worked my way down about two miles of pretty beat up roadway when my path was blocked by a pile of dirt. I could see that others had driven over it and I thought about it but I had no desire to get on the wrong side of the law in Montana and I had no reason to believe that I could reconnect with my route if I did climb over the blockage.

I turned around and considered my options as I retraced that two miles of rough pavement. I could get beyond the pile of dirt on the expressway then exit and somehow reconnect with the planned route on the other side. Or I could get beyond the pile of dirt on the expressway and just keep going. Driving to and from the blockade had made a sizable dent in the remaining daylight and reconnecting on the other side would use up even more. How much of the planned route I could actually cover before darkness set in was uncertain. What was certain was that I was tired and it would be at least 9:00 before I reached the motel regardless of my choice. I pulled onto I-90 and did not pull off until I reached Missoula.

The room was rundown and not super clean but had almost everything I needed. I say "almost" because the heat wave that would become more of an issue as I got farther west was very much in evidence, and my room had only a fan in an air conditioner housing. I'm sure it had once put out cool dry air but not while I was there. Even so, apparently I was tired enough to fall asleep.

When I decided to take to the interstate at Butte, I had accepted that I would be bypassing the Yellowstone Trail between Butte and Missoula but it bothered me. It still bothered me when I woke up in my stuffy room about 3:00 AM. It wasn't too long before I decided that, if the heat and my pending regret were going to keep me awake, I might as well do something about both of them.

Moon over Montana

The full moon was quite prominent as I retraced the previous day's I-90 dash. If my actions seem unusually crazy, maybe that moon is the reason. Before leaving the motel, I looked the map over and worked out some possible connections to my route. I would start at the first exit west of that roadblock then, if that didn't work, move west one exit and try again.

The sun was just coming up when I reached the exit. I had no problem reaching my plotted route and, feeling no time pressure, decided to see how far I could get driving east.

Roadblock (other side), Butte, MT

To my surprise, the road was clear right up to the dirt pile. Had I just driven over that hump yesterday, I could have continued merrily on my way. I now did just that while wondering what the purpose of that pile of dirt could be.

Silver Bow Creek and rails near Butte, MT

About two miles west of where I returned to the plotted route, railroad tracks running on both sides of Silver Bow Creek caught my eye. The two-lane more or less parallels I-90 at this point and I imagine I could have taken in a similar scene from the expressway if I had been looking. That's Montana Western Railway on the left and Rarus Railway on the right.

Portions of the old road have been buried under the expressway, and within a couple of miles of taking the creek and railroad picture, I was being guided back onto I-90. Had I understood that earlier, I might not have backtracked so far and accepted omitting the four or so miles of Yellowstone Trail I'd just driven. My ignorance meant I did not have to make that decision. This particular expressway stint was over in less than twenty miles. I was back on two-lane asphalt at Warm Springs, and back on gravel three miles beyond that.

I passed through small towns such as Galen, Racetrack, and Deer Lodge. In Deer Lodge, what is billed as "Montana's Best Draft Horse Show", the Big Sky Draft Horse Expo was set to open later in the day. Asphalt covered streets led through the towns while, for the most part, well-maintained gravel roads connected them.

Garrison Back Road near Garrison, MT

Approaching Garrison, on the wonderfully named Garrison Back Road, the "well maintained" portion of that description did not really apply. The road is fairly level here so the "IMPASSABLE WHEN WET" description might not be appropriate, but I'm guessing it would still be something of a challenge following any decent rain.

I was pretty happy with my decision to backtrack to pickup the old road I had bypassed in my expressway dash to Missoula, and the best was yet to come. Virtually all of the route between Garrison and Missoula was paved, and none of it would be a challenge even after a fairly big rain. In fact, several miles were, for better or worse, back on I-90. Of course it was not the I-90 portion I had in mind when I said the best was yet to come. It was the scenery beyond Drummond.

Limestone formations near Drummond, MT

The limestone cliffs in the preceding picture are about eight miles west of Drummond, Montana. The picture was taken from the I-90 frontage road and shows a bit of the Columbia River's Clark Fork separating the frontage road from the interstate which is visible on the left. About a mile later, I ducked under I-90 on Bearmouth Road and connected with Mullan Trail.

In the 1860s, the Mullan Military Road connected Fort Benton, Montana, with Walla Walla, Washington. Named after Captain John Mullan who oversaw its construction, the wagon road was quite successful but short lived. Like the Pony Express and various other wagon roads, it was pushed aside once the transcontinental railroad was completed. Sections around some of the mining towns it served were maintained by the locals but much of it fell into disrepair.

In 1914, as the Yellowstone Trail Association was working out its path to the coast, it turned to the path of Mullan Road. Between Garrison, Montana, and Spokane,

Washington, the original Yellowstone Trail roughly followed the half-century-old Mullan Military Road. It's the same corridor that now contains I-90 and US 12 and once contained US 10.

Lolo National Forest from Mullan Trail near Drummond, MT

After 160 years, the precise path of all of the Mullan Military Road is unknowable. There are sections of roads in Montana, Idaho, and Washington that bear the name Mullan that may or may not exactly follow the path established by Captain Mullan. They're probably close, however, and the above photo of Lolo National Forest across an unnamed pond would be rather scenic regardless of the name or history of the road from which it was taken.

Lolo National Forest is divided into several physically-separate sections with a combined area of two million acres. The southernmost section begins about half a mile beyond that pond. Although I would not actually enter the forest for another hundred miles, I would be surrounded by it, usually at some distance, from here to the state line. I would still be surrounded by forest after crossing the state line but its name would change.

About twenty miles beyond the pond is the town of Clinton, and Missoula is about fifteen miles beyond that. After passing through Missoula, I was not only traveling on new-to-me road but traveling through new-to-me territory.

Mullan Road near Riverbend, MT

There were a few stints on I-90 intermixed with two-lane roads with Mullan or Old Highway 10 in their names. The photo above is of Mullan Road beside Clark Fork about half a dozen miles southeast of Riverbend.

The Yellowstone Trail connected Montana and Idaho through Mullan Pass. Although some sources claim that the Mullan Road used this pass, in their book, Alice and John Ridge say this was not the case and describe the pass as mis-named. They explain that John Mullan's road went south from Mullan, Idaho, through what he named Sohon Pass. There is another Mullan Pass a dozen miles west of Helena, Montana, that Mullan Military Road did pass through.

It seems that I-90 has buried the Yellowstone Trail from DeBorgia, Montana, to near the pass. To reach the pass, I left the expressway at Exit 5 and backtracked about a mile to Randolf Creek Road.

Randolf Creek Road, MT

The road through the pass is unpaved and sometimes a little rutted and steep. But it is quite drivable and wonderfully scenic.

Summit at Mullan Pass, MT/ID

A clearing at the summit is a hub where unpaved roads and hiking trails converge, the trees change their allegiance from Lolo National Forest to Saint Joe National Forest, and the Yellowstone Trail enters Idaho.

Descending Mullan Pass into Idaho

The nearly 800 miles of Yellowstone Trail in Montana is more than in any other state and driving them made an impression on me. I believe they include examples of the full range of road surfaces and conditions present on the entire Yellowstone Trail. The Subaru Forester I was driving was equipped with something called X-Mode. It did not turn the AWD Subaru into a real off-road vehicle like a 4WD Jeep but it helped. Engine braking operation was magically altered along with other transmission characteristics. It's a feature I used multiple times in Montana. I also spent some time on the state's expressways where the speed limit was 80 miles per hour. Running at a legal 80 MPH with cruise control set closely followed by crawling at 8 MPH with X-Mode activated helped make my drive through Montana memorable.

Crossing the state line in that clearing on the summit put me in the state of Idaho for only the second time in my life. The first time had been a forty mile clip of the southeast corner that I counted for the purpose of scoring a visit to the state that I always felt a little guilty about. This time I tripled my Idaho mileage by crossing the entire state although it was at one of the narrower parts. In just over a week, I would recross the state in its widest section, add about 450 Idaho miles to my total, and completely vanquish those feelings of guilt.

Within a few miles of crossing the border, the road reaches pavement then enters the town of Mullan. On the west side of town, all traffic is forced onto I-90.

Looking east from Mullan, ID

I paused before entering Mullan to snap a picture of the road behind me and the sign alerting motorists to "LESS MAINTENANCE ON WEEKENDS AND HOLIDAYS".

Sunshine Miners Memorial, Kellogg, ID

Lead, silver, and zinc mining has long been an important industry in northern Idaho. A large statue in a roadside park east of Kellogg memorializes a disastrous 1972 fire at the Sunshine Silver Mine. A plaque below the statue of a miner with a constantly lit head lamp lists the names of the 91 miners who perished in the disaster.

Lake Coeur d'Alene and I-90 from Yellowstone Trail

At its core, Lake Coeur d'Alene is a glacier formed lake from the last ice age. Area dams have enlarged it and combined it with smaller lakes. The picture above was taken very near its eastern end and includes a bit of modern asphalt on the Yellowstone Trail and the four lanes of Interstate running between it and the lake. The lake's west end is about nine miles away and the Washington state line about nine miles beyond that.

The day's destination was less than twenty miles beyond that state line. After my sad experience at Missoula, I had booked a motel for tonight very early in the day. Spokane, Washington, had seemed like a reasonable target and I had a room waiting for me there. It's a room I would end up spending two nights in.

As I approached Washington state, I had contacted a friend living there whom I hoped to meet up with as I passed through. It was initially uncertain whether we would be able to connect but the friend, David Habura, and I had an email conversation going as I entered his state. David is a fan of old roads in general and is quite active in the Yellowstone Trail Association. His help, however, was not confined to directions and history.

The northwest U.S. was experiencing a nearly unprecedented heat wave which was going to continue, and probably get worse, over the next few days. The impact of the high temperatures on my body and car were pretty obvious but there was an indirect impact on my travels that I had not thought of. Air conditioning is rarely needed in the northwest so it is not installed in many, perhaps most, homes. The current three digit temperatures were prompting folks in those non-air-conditioned houses to visit relatives or friends or – and this is where I get concerned – move into an air-conditioned motel for a few days. The summer lodging crunch that I had already experienced was likely to get worse the farther west I traveled and the penalty for being shutout would probably get worse too. David suggested that, if I found a room with good A/C, I might want to linger there a few days through the worst of the heat wave.

My reservation in Spokane was at a mid-range chain with A/C that worked quite well. As soon as I arrived, I added three nights to my reservation.

With the backtracking and such, the last couple of days had been hectic and tiring. A break from driving was a welcome thing heatwave or not. I relaxed at the motel and the next day went out twice for meals. In between, I did laundry and contemplated my options.

Frank's Diner, Spokane, WA

Breakfast was at Frank's Diner on Second Avenue. There are two Frank's Diners in Spokane and both actually began life as railroad cars. That's something that's often claimed but seldom true. The one I visited was built by Barney & Smith in 1906 as an observation car. The other, on the north side of town, is a 1913 Laketon. Both have been added-to considerably.

Barney & Smith Manufacturing was the USA's largest builder of rail cars until Pullman took over the top spot in the early 1880s. They operated in Dayton, Ohio – about halfway between where I was born and where I now live. The company started building railroad cars in 1849 before Dayton even had a railroad. Their earliest creations left town on canal boats.

When I headed out for dinner, I had no specific restaurant targeted. I did have a brewery targeted and figured

I would either spot something on the way there or come up with something while I sampled some beer. What I had in mind was learning of something from the bartender or picking something from an internet search. It turned out to be even easier than that.

Dick's Hamburgers, Spokane, WA

As I sipped a very nice stout at Lumberbeard Brewing, I was looking at my dinner spot almost directly across the street. When the stout was gone, I walked over to Dick's Hamburgers and had a 'burger and fries at one of those sunlit tables. Yes, it was hot but there is no inside seating and the shaded tables were filled. I survived and very much enjoyed my meal. Dick's has been feeding Spokane since 1965.

Neither Frank's nor Dick's is directly on the Yellowstone but both are close. The Trail passed through Spokane on Sprague Street which is about a quarter mile north of Dick's and closer than that to Frank's.

It had been three weeks since I left home and this was the first time I had spent two consecutive nights in the same place. There was more benefit to the "day-off" than dodging the heat wave. It let me catch my breath and take stock of where I was and where I was going.

When I first reached Spokane, I had been ready to spend four days there while the heat-wave's peak came and went in Seattle. However, by the time I finished that 'burger at Dick's, I was ready to move on. During my stocktaking I had discovered a promising mom & pop motel about sixty miles west of Spokane. Before going to sleep for the second night in Spokane, I'd called the motel, spoke with the owner, decided I liked it, booked a room there, and canceled the remaining two nights at the chain. I didn't have to sit still while the heatwave punished Seattle. I could just move slowly.

US 2 (Yellowstone Trail) west of Spokane, WA

West of Spokane, two Yellowstone Trail routes exist. The earliest route goes south through Walla Walla and Yakima.

The later route goes west through Coulee City and Waterville. Although I am no longer certain of my reasons, I was planning on taking the northern route but had plotted both "just in case". My pause in Spokane gave me a chance to review this, and I did. Without an overwhelming reason to reverse it, the call made before leaving home would stand. It was even reinforced a bit by the fact that temperatures would probably be slightly higher to the south. I continued more or less straight west on the northern route.

Balancing time, temperature, and location would now be part of my travel considerations. I departed Spokane reasonably early in an effort to do whatever I was going to do before the day got really hot. Of course, heading directly to the motel I'd booked didn't make sense. It was only sixty miles away and I could easily find myself pulling in before last night's guests had checked out. My plan was to go some distance beyond the motel on older alignments then return on US 2 for check-in. Depending on how that went, I would either move on the next day or pause for another night.

Black Bear Motel, Davenport, WA

On the east edge of Davenport, the Black Bear Motel looks like a fun place to stay but it would have been an even shorter drive and the faux wild west town is pretty much just for show. It houses the motel's office but the rooms are in a normal looking one story building across the way.

On the other side of Davenport, I followed a couple segments of old road. They were signed "PRIMITIVE ROAD" but were well maintained graded gravel and much less primitive than several roads I'd driven in Montana.

Primitive road west of Creston, WA

I had a leisurely breakfast at a locally owned restaurant in Creston then found a road that tried much harder to live up to its "primitive" designation but it was still pretty tame. I'm talking about Hills Road heading off into the distance on the right side of the photo above.

Despite the leisurely breakfast and slow driving, I reached Wilbur, where my room awaited, well before noon. I continued on older alignments knowing that I could backtrack to Wilbur then return to the turnaround point relatively quickly on the current US 2.

Banks Lake, Coulee City, WA

Of course, not everything I drove was a narrow old alignment. Modern US 2 was frequently the only way forward and that included crossing Banks Lake at Coulee City. The crossing provided a demonstration of the powerful temperature control inherent in large bodies of water.

With the northwest heatwave a common news topic, I was watching the car's temperature readout almost as closely as the speedometer. I was quite comfortable in my climate-controlled cocoon but the readout kept me aware of what was going on outside the car and what sort of punishment I could expect if a breakdown occurred. It had been slowly climbing throughout the morning and had reached 98° F somewhere east of Coulee City. As I approached the lake it began to slowly drop then plummeted as I actually passed the water. By the time it started to rise again on the other side, it had bottomed out at 83° F. That fifteen degree drop happened in less than two minutes.

About twenty miles west of Coulee City, I found a closed gate across an old Yellowstone Trail alignment I had planned on driving. The five mile segment, along Baseline Road, was now inside McCartney Creek Preserve and a sign declared it available to "Foot Traffic Only". Had the temperature and/or my age been lower by thirty or so, I might have considered it but not today.

Waterville Hotel, Waterville, WA

The town of Waterville with its historic Waterville Hotel lies about fifteen miles beyond the off-limits Baseline Road. The 1903 hotel had been high on my list of desirable places to stay but was, as explained by a sign on one of those pillars, "TEMPORARILY CLOSED DUE TO COVID". Even before I knew that, I had dropped it as an active candidate because of a lack of air conditioning capable of handing the current heatwave and a location I thought too far from Spokane for my first test night west of the city and too close for the second. I was obviously wrong in dropping it because of location since it would have been a perfect first stop out of Spokane if I'd been a little more ambitious. We will never know if a decision based on temperature would have been any more accurate as the COVID-based closure saved me from making any decision at all.

The hotel has embraced multiple colors of named auto trails. That painted white frame on the building's side wall surrounds a faded but original Red Trail logo. The Red Trail was a nation-wide auto trail with one end in Seattle and the other in New York City.

US 2 east of Orondo, WA

Baseline road had been my last planned venture off of US 2 and the Waterville Hotel had been the last point of interest I'd planned to spend some time looking over. I was now free to scurry back to Wilbur and return directly to Waterville in the morning without any sightseeing diversions. But I would still arrive early and the day was going well so I decided to keep going a bit longer and discovered that US 2 west of Waterville is, despite being divided four-lane, a very scenic stretch of highway. Knowing that I would be driving through this again the next day didn't bother me a bit.

1908 Columbia River Bridge, Wenatchee, WA

I actually made it to Wenatchee and past the 1908 Columbia River Bridge. The bridge is open to pedestrians but my comment at Baseline Road about too many degrees and too many years now applied doubly. A drive-by photo satisfied me completely.

A large water pipe occupies about half of the bridge's deck. I assumed that was added when the bridge stopped carrying vehicles. Not so, I learned. The bridge was built by a canal company primarily for carrying water across the river to apple orchards. Carrying horse drawn wagons and the occasional automobile was a bonus. The large pipe inside the structure merely replaced a pair of smaller pipes that had been attached to its sides since day one.

I turned around at Wenatchee to return to Wilbur. The next three pictures are in the correct order chronologically but not geographically.

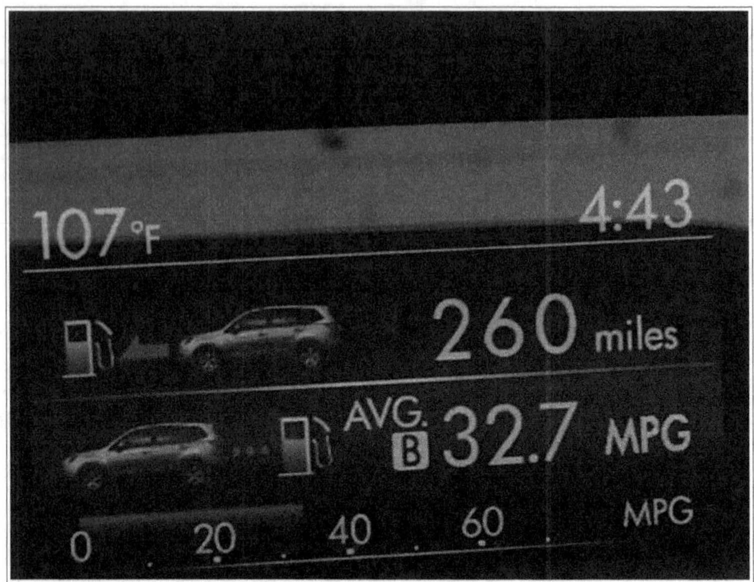

Temperature west of Wilbur, WA

I snapped a picture of the temperature about twenty-five miles from Wilbur but it was not done climbing.

Willows Motel, Wilbur, WA

The Willows was my haven for the night.

Billy Burgers, Wilbur, WA

Dinner was at Billy Burgers, which I had noticed and snapped a picture of while westbound. It is only about a thousand feet from the Willows but I have to confess to driving there rather than walking. I'll also confess to failing to get a picture of the temperature on that short drive. The readout in the car said 116° F but the official temperature from a nearby radio station was only 112. Officially, I probably couldn't tell the difference.

In the morning, I pulled onto US 2 and cruised through Waterville and the wonderful scenery beyond – blissfully unaware that a mistake I'd made months before was about to catch up with me. I may have even enjoyed the view more the second time than I had the first because I had no need to watch for turnoffs or stop to read signs at closed gates. After reaching Wenatchee, I left US 2 a few times to drive short sections of older alignments then left it permanently to drive south on US 97. I drove a couple of narrow asphalt-covered older alignments as I approached and entered Wenatchee National Forest. Several miles inside the forest, I turned onto

Old Blewett Pass Highway which looked to be more of the same. That's where that old mistake snagged me although I did not realize it at the time.

Old Blewett Pass Highway, Wenatchee National Forest

It was the taming of Blewett Pass in 1925 that allowed the Yellowstone Trail to switch from the southern route through Walla Walla to this shorter northern route. US 97 avoids the grades and switchbacks of Blewett Pass Highway by curving around the pass. The highway is still there and is now paved and, although it is significantly more time consuming than US 97, a very pleasant and scenic drive. Or so I've heard. Less than a mile after turning onto Old Blewett Pass Highway, I turned off of it just like my GPS instructed.

The way routes are plotted basically involves picking two points, letting routing software plot a course between them, then adding intermediate points as necessary. When I plotted my path through Blewett Pass, I started with two points on US 97 then went no further. Roads the size of those in Blewett Pass can only be seen on rather high resolution maps.

On computers, that usually means a high zoom level. It seems not to have occurred to me that there could be more than one path through Blewett Pass so when my routing software (Garmin BaseCamp) plotted a path through the space inside US 97's curve, I called it good. Had I simply zoomed in enough to see that multiple choices existed I might have then studied it sufficiently to sort things out. As it was, I turned off of the paved road to follow what Garmin had determined to be the shortest path through the pass.

Forest Service Road 7320-200, Wenatchee National Forest

That path was on service roads which were essentially Jeep trails. It eventually sunk in that this couldn't be right when the GPS wanted me to drive over a drop-off that would have been somewhat of a challenge in a real Jeep and was totally ridiculous in a Subaru Forester – even one with X-Mode on. In true "fish story" tradition, you should have seen the road I didn't get pictures of.

Once I stopped following the voice in the box, I was basically directionless. Fortunately, as it turned out, there were no choices to be made and about a mile later I saw some pavement through the trees. A couple of men in a small parking area helped me get my bearings.

Forest Service Road 9715, Wenatchee National Forest

Forest Service Road 9715, Wenatchee National Forest

As it turned out, I was actually at the south end of Old Blewett Pass Highway where it connects to Forest Service Road 9715. This was the path I should have been on all along. That knowledge made the forest views a little prettier and the hairpin turns significantly friendlier. It took about fifteen minutes to reach US 97 but more than a day to figure out what went wrong.

A few miles later, the two Yellowstone Trail alignments that separated near Spokane rejoined. US 97 continued south to form part of the southern route while I turned west toward Seattle.

Immediately after passing through a chip and seal operation in South Cle Elum, a long crack magically appeared in my windshield. Although I can't be certain, it seems likely that it came from an airborne rock in the work zone. Whatever the cause, I now had something new to look at for the rest of the trip.

I had made a reservation at the Summit Inn in Snoqualmie Pass from my room in Wilbur. I reached the inn without further incident, but things were a bit hectic there and my room wasn't exactly waiting for me. The room was eventually ready, and I spent a comfortable night sleeping while the crack in my windshield grew a little longer.

In the morning, I was surprised to learn that the next few miles of Yellowstone Trail were one-way eastbound. That wasn't a major problem since the old road was paralleled by I-90 and I just had to drive to the next exit then drive back. I assume that the road's narrowness and twists are the reason that it is now one-way. That probably also accounts for it being closed in the winter.

I was aware of an original Yellowstone Trail marker painted on a stone along this road although I didn't know exactly where. For lack of a better excuse, I blame the confusion caused by the one-way road interfering with my plotted route for making me forget to look.

Denny Creek Road, Snoqualmie Pass, WA

I now believe that I might have seen the stone had I just looked to the right around the time I was taking the preceding picture of the bridge.

Meadowbrook Bridge, Snoqualmie, WA

In Snoqualmie, traffic lights keep vehicles on the 1921 Meadowbrook Bridge to a single lane.

Red Brick Road near Redmond, WA

The westbound Yellowstone Trail continues the northwest slant begun near Cle Elum until it clears the north end of Lake Sammamish. Near the lake's northeast corner is a stretch of original Yellowstone Trail called, for obvious reasons, The Red Brick Road. Red bricks used to pave the road in 1913 continue to support the road's traffic. Not surprisingly, some users of the road want to cover it with asphalt and raise the speed limit but so far they have been held off. The road's official name is 196th Avenue but The Red Brick Road is a lot more popular.

When the Yellowstone Trail was in its prime, motorists crossed Washington Lake on a ferry connecting Kirkland Avenue with Madison Street but no ferries have crossed the lake since 1951. I paid a visit to the foot of Kirkland Avenue on the lake's east side but did not visit its west shore counterpart at Madison Street. I crossed the lake on I-90 and picked up the Yellowstone Trail on Jackson Street.

Pioneer Square, Seattle, WA

I documented my arrival at the terminus in Pioneer Square by taking a picture through the passenger side window. A city police cruiser blocked my view of the park but left no doubt as to where the picture was taken.

Following my drive-by of the square, I found a parking lot and walked back. My extra night in Spokane and my unhurried pace since then had paid off. The temperature in Seattle had reached 106° F on the day before I arrived. On this day the high would be in the low 90s. I walked slowly, of course, but I could at least get some better photos of Pioneer Square and briefly relish my completion of the Yellowstone Trail. Had it been 106, I may not have even left the car.

Pioneer Square. Seattle, WA

I don't doubt that opinions will vary on whether or not I was successful in getting a better picture of Pioneer Square. There is no police car blocking half of it, and it does include the large totem pole, which is possibly the square's most recognizable feature., but there is also an abundance of tents where some of the city's homeless are living. I'm not trying to make a statement; merely document reality. It's a sad situation that is not confined to a single city or to the terminus of one historic highway.

From the square, I walked to the waterfront for a little celebration. Maybe hot soup on a 90 degree day isn't everybody's idea of a celebration but a cup of Ivar's clam chowder was exactly what I'd been looking forward to when I reached Seattle, and I very much enjoyed it despite the temperature.

Then I was back in the air-conditioned car and out of the city.

8.   Down the Other Coast

Moving between US 20 and the Yellowstone Trail on the east coast took less than two hours and barely got a mention in this book. Moving between them on the west coast gets its own chapter. One reason is that they are farther apart – 220 miles vs. 35 miles. But more importantly, there were people and places on the west coast that I wanted to visit. All together, the result is a sort of intermission: a chapter dealing with travel on neither US 20 nor the Yellowstone Trail.

David Habura and me, Tumwater, WA

On the morning after reaching the western end of the Yellowstone Trail, I met up with David Habura in Tumwater Historical Park. A few years back, David guided me around the Columbia River Gorge area, and on this trip he provided lots of insight into the Yellowstone Trail and weather in Washington state. In between he has helped me with a variety of information from his collection of historical maps and guide books. Today be brought coffee and muffins.

Former Olympia Brewery, Tumwater, WA

The building behind us is the former Olympia Brewery. The state of Washington rushed ahead of the rest of the country by making alcoholic beverages illegal in 1916 which is the last year that beer was brewed in this building. Brewing did resume after prohibition but it was in a new building. The old brewhouse had other tenants for a time but the building sat empty for many years. The city of Tumwater is currently involved in a project to restore it.

David brought more than coffee and muffins, of course. He brought his knowledge of local roads and that saved me from a day spent entirely on expressways. My next target was Portland, Oregon, but I had not spent any time planning on how to get there.

Old US 99, Bucoda, WA

David suggested Old US 99, and, even though time constraints obliged me to move onto I-5 at Centralia, I had very nice two-lane to that point.

Deschutes Brewery Public House, Portland, OR

There was also a brewery involved in my second meeting of the day but this one was very much still in business. I like to visit breweries and Portland has a bunch of them. I asked Cece Otto, the person I was meeting, to pick one, and she suggested Deschutes.

Me, Dan, and Cece, Portland, OR

Although he missed the first round, Cece's husband, Dan, did break free and joined us for the last one.

Cece is a singer who presents history through song. We first met when she was performing early twentieth century travel-related songs in celebration of the Lincoln Highway's centennial. She has since done programs on World War I and Women's Suffrage centennials. Find her at AmericanSongline.com.

There was one more item on my list of things to do before turning east. This was only my second time in the state of Oregon, and one of the things I remembered fondly from my 2008 visit was the scenic coast. I left Portland headed toward the coast's nearest point to get in the maximum amount of ocean-side driving on the way to the start/end of US 20 in Newport, Oregon. My plan was to drive US 26 to the beginning of OR-6 then take the state highway to Tillamook. I turned onto US 26 at the eastern end of the section officially named Sunset Highway. But just before reaching OR-6, a sign giving mileage to Seaside triggered a memory.

In 2008, timing prevented me from eating at the original location of the highly-recommended Pig 'N Pancake restaurant in Seaside. I had settled for the Astoria outpost. Today, on seeing the mileage sign, I immediately decided to head for the original, and rolled right past the OR-6 turnoff. I'm sure glad I did. Not only did I have a great breakfast, I got my best pictures of the Oregon coast between Seaside and Tillamook.

Arcadia Beach, OR

The Oregon coastline is not filled with sunlit sandy beaches like those found in Florida or southern California.

The words that frequently come to mind when thinking of the coast in Oregon are "rugged" and "misty".

Oswald West State Park, OR

Rugged and misty might not always translate to scenic, but they certainly seem to in Oregon.

9.   From the Other Coast

US 20 sign, Newport, OR

This is the mate of the big green sign that I almost – but not quite – reached in Boston twenty-two days ago. It would probably make better reading if I really was about to travel 3,365 miles to the other end of Route 20 but the truth is that I only needed to drive about 2,500 miles to reach the point in Ohio where I had turned east on US 20 on the very first day of the trip.

Of course, the 2,500 miles I would be driving and the first three-quarters of the miles referred to by the sign are not the exact same miles. The sign's miles are measured along the current official routing of US 20. The miles I would be driving are on earlier alignments of Historic Route 20.

US 20 was one of the initial batch of United States Numbered Highways created in 1926 but it initially ended at the eastern edge of Yellowstone National Park. That means the earliest alignments west of the park date from 1940, when it was extended to Albany, Oregon, and 1943, when it was extended to the coast. Because US Highways are not signed inside of national parks, US 20 officially has a big gap in Wyoming but the mileage of the road inside the park is included in calculating its length.

The first separation of eastbound old and new occurs rather quickly. Less than half a mile from that big green sign the historic route splits to the north of the current route while the current alignment maintains a fairly solid eastern direction with wide lanes and gentle curves. The curves it replaced are more numerous and less gentle and the lanes – or more often, lane – are not as wide.

Valley Ridge Drive, Newport, OR

The old road around Newport has been chopped up considerably over the years. Although I tried, I could not drive it all. Some was blocked off due, presumably, to its condition.

Valley Ridge Lane, Newport, OR

And some because it is now on private land.

Pleasant Valley Road near Sweet Home, OR

Additional sections of the original alignment east of Newport were bypassed as the route was improved but these seem less fragmented and were clearly better maintained. This was probably for the benefit of local traffic. I tend to overuse the word "pleasant" in describing drives on well-maintained roads away from development, but there is official support for applying that description to a nearly-ten-mile-long uninterrupted section of older alignment between South Lebanon and Sweet Home. About half of it is now signed Pleasant Valley Road.

US 20 in Williamette National Forest, OR

Of course, the scenery that helps make Pleasant Valley Road pleasant also looks good on non-bypassed sections of US 20 – even when enhanced with multiple lanes and fancy signage. The overhead sign in the preceding photo reminds us of the danger that we humans present to that great scenery we are driving through.

That rugged coast and those tree-lined hills and valleys with thin bands of pavement weaving through them are definitely scenic but Oregon has more. It has 50 named mountain ranges and more than 3,500 mountains. The highest, at 11,249 feet, is Mount Hood which I saw on my 2008 visit.

Mount Washington, OR

This is Mount Washington in the Cascade Range. US 20 passes about a half dozen miles away and a pull-off almost directly north of the peak offers an unobstructed view. It looks pretty big to me but its elevation of 7,798 feet doesn't even make the top thirty in Oregon. It barely made the top thirty in prominence (height above surroundings) at 2,574 feet compared to Mount Hood's 7,706 feet. The competition is tough.

The city of Bend, Oregon, is about thirty-five miles past Mount Washington. This is where the Deschutes production brewery and main tasting room is located. Despite the tasting room not being directly on US 20 and having visited the Portland outpost two days earlier, I could not let this opportunity slip by. I just sampled a couple of beers but one of those was Black Butte XXXIII which had been brewed specifically to celebrate the brewery's thirty-third anniversary on the Sunday preceding my visit.

It seems US 20 in Oregon satisfied all of its rerouting needs on the western side of the state. After leaving Bend, I did not leave the current US 20 until near the Idaho line, and when I did it was not to pursue an earlier US 20 alignment but to see something much older.

I drove around the town of Vale for a bit, looking over some murals and the town's oldest building. The 1872 structure seems kind of new compared to buildings on the east end of Twenty but it is the local record holder and houses the town's museum. At the museum I learned of the Keeney Pass Interpretive Site where remnants of the Oregon Trail can be seen about six miles south of town.

Oregon Trail, Keeney Pass Interpretive Site, Vale, OR

The Oregon Trail was the path that migrants used to reach Oregon from the Missouri River Valley in the mid-nineteenth century. It was never paved, signed, or otherwise intentionally marked in any way. What I referred to as "remnants" are the ruts made by thousands of feet and wagon wheels.

Silver Bridge, Caldwell, ID

The first time I left the current US 20 alignment in Idaho was when it decided to piggy-back on the I-84 expressway. I followed Old Highway 20 over the Boise River and through downtown Caldwell. The river crossing was on the 1922 Silver Bridge which I'm guessing was a little shinier when given its name. I returned to the current US 20 when it left the expressway on the other side of Caldwell.

There are two places in Idaho where the current route of US 20 has been shortened quite a bit from its 1940 path. One is between the towns of Mountain Home and Carey, and the other is between Butte City and Idaho Falls. I, of course, followed the longer route in both cases.

South of Boise, everything is funneled onto I-84 including me and Historic Route 20. I-84 then bypasses Mountain Home, and mid-bypass US 20 splits from the interstate to head directly east. I followed Old Highway 30 right through Mountain Home.

Yes, the older road through here is signed Old Highway 30, not 20. Remember that in the US Highways scheme officially adopted in 1926, US 20 ended at Yellowstone National Park while US 30 went all the way to the Pacific Coast. This had not been the case in the plan proposed a year earlier. In that preliminary offering, US 20 continued through the park and on to the coast at Astoria, Oregon, and US 30 ended at Salt Lake City, Utah. Among several problems associated with that approach was the fact that, at the time, Yellowstone National Park was closed for six months of each year. The solution was to end US 20 at the park and extend US 30 to Astoria. At roughly the same longitude as US 20's encounter with Yellowstone Park, US 30 turns away from Salt Lake City and towards the northwest. It's kind of like a tackled football runner launching a lateral pass just before hitting the ground. Yellowstone National Park tackled US 20 and US 30 had to get the football to Astoria, Oregon.

This should help explain what, depending on how much is known about highway numbering, seems a major goof on the west coast. US Highway numbers are supposed to increase from north to south and east to west. Interstate highways are to follow the reverse pattern. There are exceptions, of course, as geographic features force highways together and even across each other, but that's not exactly why these two major routes, ending in zeroes, are out of sequence at their termini. US 30's fourteen-year head start meant that when US 20 did head for the coast, it had to cross US 30 to get there.

That crossing occurs in Idaho. It was not accomplished with a simple crossroad intersection and it did not happen instantly. Between Caldwell and Yellowstone National Park,

US 30 and early US 20 shared quite a bit of roadway. Sometimes it was official and sometimes it was only temporary until construction of the designated US 20 route could be completed.

Old Highway 30, UP RR, & Snake River near King Hill, ID

Eastbound Old Highway 30 never rejoins I-84 although it stays fairly close for quite some ways. It also stays fairly close to the Snake River and the Union Pacific Railroad as seen in the picture above.

Finding places to sleep was certainly playing a bigger role in this trip than it should have. Having freshly relearned a lesson with the Butte/Missoula fiasco, I was really trying to book a room no later than very early morning on the day I needed it. Booking it the day before was even better. Everything was certainly not completely back to normal but it was clear that a significant percentage of Americans were trying to make up for stay-cations that COVID-19 had forced on them in 2020. Of course, the situation was amplified when the day in question was a Saturday and Independence

Day Eve. I found absolutely nothing directly on my route but did come up with something less than ten miles off of it.

I-84 comes into Bliss, Idaho, carrying the current US 26 and US 30. It leaves with neither of them. US 26, which is also Historic Route 20 at this point, heads east while US 30 and I-84 head south and southeast respectively. I turned onto US 30 and headed to my room in Hagerman.

I had never before used the service the motel was booked through, and I was slightly nervous about it. Things couldn't have been better. Both the motel (Hagerman Valley Inn) and the restaurant next door (Snake River Grill) were independently owned and essentially what I always hope to find. Even the off-route drive, which was the booking's only downside, was really enjoyable. The Snake River had turned south with US 30 and there was some excellent scenery as it skirted Hagerman Fossil Beds National Monument.

US 20 near Craters of the Moon National Monument, ID

I was quickly back on route in the morning, and roughly sixty miles after that had rejoined the current US 20 which was doing triple duty at that point. About twenty-five miles after rejoining US 20, I pulled into Craters of the Moon National Monument.

Craters of the Moon National Monument, ID

The park's website describes it as "a vast ocean of lava flows with scattered islands of cinder cones and sagebrush". It is best experienced on foot. Some of the trails are short and level to make that easy. I parked and started out on one of these but quickly turned back. My earlier comment about requiring thirty less degrees of temperature or years of age for outside activity was also true here. The temperature at Craters of the Moon might be a few degrees less than it was at the closed road in Washington but it was still in the mid-90s and I had not become one minute younger. I returned to the car and finished driving the 7-mile Loop Road. My loss.

I confess that I'm not entirely certain that, before today, I would have answered correctly if asked what state Craters of the Moon was in. But I'm confident I could have named the state with a potato museum.

Idaho Potato Museum, Blackfoot, ID

The Idaho Potato Museum in Blackfoot has exhibits on all things potato and a cafe with a potato themed menu. Huckleberry flavored potato ice cream is mighty good.

Uniroyal Gal, Blackfoot, ID

I had to backtrack a couple of blocks from the museum then go about a half mile off course to photograph the Uniroyal Gal in front of Martha's Cafe but it was so worth it. She once balanced a big plate of French fries in her raised left hand but took a little vacation in 2011 and returned with a big engagement ring and no fries.

I did no planning for Independence Day but naively assumed that there would be something going on wherever I landed at the end of the day. That landing turned out to be in Idaho Falls.

Idaho Falls advertises "the largest Independence Day fireworks show west of the Mississippi River". Unfortunately for me, that show occurred on Saturday, July 3. The Fourth of July in Idaho Falls felt exactly like what it was: the day after a huge party. Everyone was at home recovering and even finding a place open to eat was a challenge. I ended up getting food from a drive-thru and eating in my room. Pops from a few random firecrackers could be heard from my room but my Independence Day was bizarrely quiet.

A Peter Toth Whispering Giant, Idaho Falls, ID

I paused to photograph the Whispering Giant on Historic Route 20/US 26 as I was leaving Idaho Falls the next morning. This member of Peter Wolf Toth's "Trail of the Whispering Giants" was carved in 1980.

Outdoor museum near Rexburg, ID

A short time later, I was photographing an outdoor museum of sorts created by someone who appears to be quite a Conoco fan.

On the east side of Idaho Falls, US 20's historic and current alignments come together. In places they are one and the same and at others they are merely close. For example, the collection of artifacts I've called an outdoor museum is on an older alignment where the current US 20 is a divided four-lane about 75 yards away.

At the town of Ashton, the old and new move a bit farther apart for several miles. Both routes go through Targhee National Forest but the current alignment runs more or less due north while the older alignment curves to the east to follow Henry's Fork of the Snake River.

Cabin near Warm River, ID

The cabin pictured above is on a tributary of Henry's Fork named Warm River. The nearby town of Warm River is Idaho's least populated with just three residents in the 2020 census. The seagull perched on the railing is a worthy guardian of the cabin. After taking my photos, I had to wait as it strutted down the road before I could pull out.

Lower Mesa Falls, Targhee National Forest, ID

Targhee National Forest begins just beyond that cabin, and it offers plenty of scenery with several opportunities to pause and enjoy it. The preceding photo of Lower Mesa Falls on Henry's Fork was taken from an overlook built by the Civilian Conservation Corps. Targhee National Forest abuts Yellowstone National Park with little more than a state line separating the two. That "little more" is the two miles of Yellowstone Park that extends west into Idaho and Montana.

There's also a little more than a state line that separates Idaho from Wyoming when traveling US 20. Reminding me of the thirteen miles of Kansas that US 66 traversed, US 20 spends about ten miles in Montana. I don't have much evidence that I was even in the state.

West Yellowstone Rodeo, MT

There is one picture of a rodeo site a couple of miles beyond the Idaho-Montana state line and another of the

West Yellowstone, MT

congestion at the Yellowstone Park entrance. Then I was inside the park and inside Wyoming.

I'm sure it seems absurd to many to think of simply driving straight through Yellowstone National Park but that was my plan. I had dealt with the crowds in order to watch Old Faithful do its thing back in 2014 and felt no need to do that again. Of course, I had no illusions of sailing through the park as if it wasn't there. It is one of the country's most popular parks, and it was the day after Independence Day during a summer when attendance records were being threatened at several national parks. Plus there is just so much beauty that it is impossible to avoid pausing at least a few times to photograph or simply admire it.

Madison River, Yellowstone NP, WY

Firehole River, Yellowstone NP, WY

I tried to pause where other people didn't. There are plenty of mountains, streams, meadows, and even geysers to go around.

Some closures and construction diverted me from what I had decided was the most direct path through the park, and either those diversions or my misunderstanding of them led me to drive through the Old Faithful parking lot. It was absolutely packed and simultaneously reinforced my decision to expedite my passage through the park and prevented me from doing it.

Clouds had covered the sky all day, and they split open not long after I made it through the Old Faithful lot. I had seen people working their way through that giant lot and standing in line at park restaurants which allowed me to put faces on some of the people I knew were getting drenched by the rain.

Old Faithful is toward the western side of the park meaning I was less than halfway through when the rain hit. It did lighten up before long but did not stop completely until I was nearly out of the park. I couldn't help but feel sorry for families that had traveled multiple days to reach the park and get soaked.

Yellowstone Lake, Yellowstone NP, WY

Of course, I took a lot more than two pictures in the park. That included some very sad and unscenic ones of the fire damage at the north end of Yellowstone Lake.

Shoshone National Forest, WY

US 20 goes straight from Yellowstone National Park to Shoshone National Forest without even a slight pause in scenery.

Smith Mansion, Cody, WY

And some of the scenery in man made.

I have not learned exactly when construction of this house on a hill twenty miles west of Cody started but I know when it stopped. That was in 1992 when Francis Lee Smith, who single-handedly built the house, fell to his death while working on the building's second story. His obsession with the house had already done in his marriage. Smith's wife divorced him in the 1980s. Working backward, it seems he must have started working on the house around 1979 or '80.

Calling it a mansion is more than a stretch. There is no electricity and the only heat source is a small wood burning stove. I don't know about water. In late 2019, it was sold to the owners of a nearby RV park who, at the time, weren't quite sure what they were going to do with it. They might not be any surer today.

US 14/16/20 tunnel near Cody, WY

Getting to Cody, Wyoming, from Yellowstone National Park involves a group of three tunnels just a few miles west of the city. The tunnels were built in 1960 when the road was relocated. The first tunnel (pictured) is the longest in the state at 3,202 feet. The second and third are 267 and 196 feet in length respectively. Buffalo Bill Reservoir is just out of frame to the right.

Millstone Pizza Company, Cody, WY

In Cody, I reached a milestone at Millstone. Millstone Pizza Company & Brewery had been on my radar since before the trip started. A friend and his wife had eaten here a few years ago and thought it the best pizza they ever had. It was at the end of a long drive and they were famished and eventually got to wondering just how much their elevated appetites affected their judgment. I try to avoid any absolute statements so won't declare this the best pizza I ever had. On the other hand, I won't rule out the possibility.

I was not at all surprised by the quality of the pizza but I did get a big surprise at Millstone. I track the breweries I visit and was quite proud of reaching 200 a couple of years ago. I knew I was getting close to 300 but not exactly how close. Very close, it turns out, and this was it.

Antler Motel, Greybull, WY

I quite enjoyed my night at the Antler Motel in Greybull although I was in a standard room and not one of those cute cabins in the picture.

US 20's heading varies frequently as it moves from the coast through Oregon and most of Idaho. At Blackfoot, Idaho, it strikes out on a fairly straight northeast course to clip the corner of Montana and enter Yellowstone National Park. Exiting the park, it heads due east to Greybull where it drops sharply south to roughly the latitude where the climb to the north started in Blackfoot. At Shoshoni, it joins US 26 to resume its steady run to the east. The drive between Greybull and Shoshoni is a real treat.

When I wrote the word "treat" I was thinking of the area's natural features but there are some man-made treats along the way too.

Trucks and tractors south of Manderson, WY

About ten miles south of Manderson, I passed by a collection of trucks and tractors that easily topped any of those collections of Pontiacs and other cars I saw in Minnesota, South Dakota, and Montana. The picture above shows just a tiny bit of the array of trucks, tractors, and other vehicles that stretched for more than a quarter-mile along the road and in places was two and three rows deep. I naturally wanted to pull over but I was in a long line of traffic following a pilot car through a construction zone, and decided that would not be wise.

This picture, and the ones I took of rusting cars while headed west, might make it seem like I'm making a case for the advancement of junk yards. That's not exactly true. I fully understand that junk cars do not make America beautiful but, in certain situations, they can make it interesting.

"Pioneer Canal Digger", Worland, WY

"Pioneer Canal Digger" is one of several Lyndon Fayne Pomeroy sculptures in Worland's Pioneer Square.

Old US 20 near Winchester, WY

Between Worland and Thermopolis, I made it onto a couple of sections of old roadway. The first bypasses the town of Winchester and returns to the current US 20 after about two miles.

Old US 20 near Kirby, WY

The second actually goes through the town of Kirby but trails off onto private land about a mile south of town. A tiny black speck near the center of the picture is a hand-painted "PRIVATE" sign hanging from concrete bridge railings and blocking the road. Driving back to Kirby was required to return to US 20.

With a population around 3,000, Thermopolis is Hot Spring County's largest city. The city and county both get their names from what is said to be the "WORLD'S LARGEST MINERAL HOT SPRING". White painted rocks on a hillside overlooking the spring are arranged to say exactly that in forming what must be one of the world's largest advertisements.

The Big Spring, Thermopolis, WY

The Big Spring is part of Hot Springs State Park at the north edge of Thermopolis. The picture was taken from an overlook on US 20 that offers some very nice views.

Howie at Discover Thermopolis, Thermopolis, WY

The spring isn't the only hot thing in Thermopolis nor are it and the sign the only "largest" things in town. Discover Thermopolis advertises its selection of 1800 hot sauces as the largest in the nation. It's a gift and souvenir store with a lot of variety. (I got a memory card for my camera there.) Owner Howie Samelson is a knowledgeable fan of old roads in general and Historic US 20 in particular.

Old cars and roads, hot sauce and water, and life size metal horses are certainly enough treats to justify my claim but there's more. South of Thermopolis, US 20 enters the Wind River Indian Reservation and passes through Wind River Canyon.

Wind River Canyon, WY

Most of US 20's time in the canyon is spent hugging the east side of the Wind River while the Burlington Northern Santa Fe Railroad hugs the other side.

Tunnels in Wind River Canyon, WY

As it passes through the canyon, US 20 encounters another set of three tunnels although these are much shorter than the trio seen just west of Cody. The picture above shows the middle of the three automobile tunnels with the entrance of a railroad visible across the river.

Boysen State Park and Boysen Reservoir are less than a mile south of the tunnels. Construction of Boysen Dam, which created the reservoir, began in 1946 and was completed in 1952. Part of the project involved moving several miles of railroad and auto road to the east.

US 20 finishes its southern "correction" at Shoshoni and turns east. The current and historic alignment are mostly, but not always, the same. In Casper and Douglas, I took the old alignment through the towns as the modern Route Twenty bypassed them.

Old US 20 near Manville, WY

To be honest, I believe I have included the photo of the former US 20 two-track headed into Manville as much to show off the Wyoming clouds as the little-used road.

American Legion Post No. 1 sign, Van Tassell, WY

Van Tassell, Wyoming, is about a mile from the Nebraska border. That's close enough that it appears to be right on the line on most maps. I used it as a motel search target when I thought I would be ending a day near the state line. Everything that turned up was at least several miles away and when I reached the town it was immediately obviously why. The town limit sign shows a population of 15.

But it was once 170, and the town was once home to American Legion Post Number 1. A wooden interpretive sign marks the spot. Reading the sign made me think of those pictures that show a feeble old man seeing the reflection of a vigorous young soldier in the mirror or a bent and stooped old-timer casting the shadow of a sturdy upright young man. Some places might not look like much today but just about every one has a story worth hearing.

As I explained when entering Montana on the Yellowstone Trail, the north-south line defining the eastern borders of Montana and Wyoming also defines my own idea of the start/end of the American West although that border is a lot less precise than the state borders. That means that, as I now exited Wyoming, I felt I was also exiting the West. More importantly, perhaps, I felt that I was no longer traveling away from the Pacific Ocean so much as toward the Great Lakes.

10. Back to the Center

Nebraska has the normal mixture of old and current alignments of US 20. Roughly twenty miles of the old unpaved route exists between the towns of Crawford and Chadron.

Old and older US 20 near Whitney, NE

In the picture above, it is the older alignment running straight ahead. Although I've been known to drive similar looking roadways from time to time, I did not drive this one. Many factors might determine whether or not I take off on a primitive looking road, and they include my mood at the time. Maybe I just didn't feel like it. Looking at the picture, I'm thinking that double-headed arrow, on what was basically a T intersection, might have had something to do with my decision.

About half way across the state, a gravel section just east of Valentine gave me multiple reasons to remember it. First off, it was extremely well maintained. Second, by virtue of passing through the Fort Niobrara National Wildlife Refuge, it was extremely scenic. It had speed limit and curve signs neither of which is all that common on unpaved roads. Then, just after exiting the refuge, it had something I don't recall ever seeing on an unpaved road. It was one of those "truck on a wedge" signs warning of a steep descent. That descent led to the Niobrara River and a hundred year old bridge looking as well maintained as the road it was on.

1920 Berry Bridge, Niobrara River, near Sparks, NE

A canoe livery operates at the north end of the bridge so there may be some connection between the business and the level of road maintenance. A couple of miles beyond the bridge, I got to see some of that maintenance, and Nebraska courtesy, in real-time.

Grader on Berry Bridge Road near Sparks, NE

I encounter road graders on gravel and dirt roads more than you might imagine, and wasn't very surprised when I came upon one after crossing the Niobrara. In fact, given the condition of the road, I probably should have assumed one was operating somewhere along it nearly full time. My standard procedure is to tag along at some distance until the grader turns onto another road or the road become wide enough for me to pass. I have turned around a time or two but it's rare. Even rarer is having the operator pull off to the side and stop to let me get by. So far that's happened once. This was that time.

I had turned onto the gravel Berry Bridge Road from NE 12 and I was back on it shortly after passing the grader. Just before reaching Sparks, I left the pavement to follow some section-line "stair steps" that the modern road had bypassed. About three miles west of Springview, I left NE 12 one last time for what turned out to be a minor misadventure.

General store, Meadville, NE

The winding gravel road passed through some scenic countryside on the way to Meadville where the former post office and general store is now a bar and grill. Unfortunately, that green light in the window is a "CLOSED" sign. The Niobrara River runs nearby and I've since learned that a "Polar Bear Plunge" has been held there the last few years in January.

After one more series of curves south of Meadville, my plot showed a straight shot south to Ainsworth and the current US 20. On this particular day, that turned out to be not quite right.

Former US 20 near Ainsworth, NE

The road was definitely straight but, about seven miles north of Ainsworth, it was closed. A pickup truck in front of me turned right and I probably should have followed. However, based on my intended path being south and east, I turned left.

More closures were encountered at an intersection two miles later but there was no decision to to be made. Roads to both the south and east were blocked, and I found myself just one turn shy of driving in circles. I was now stepping northeast on section lines. With a sigh of relief, I reached US 183, and that straight shot south, in just a few more miles.

There was more gravel and more stair steps to be driven in Nebraska but none, fortunately, after I encountered rain around Atkinson. Rain and unpaved roads can sometimes be a truly unpleasant combination although my guess is that most of the unpaved roads I was on in Nebraska could handle a fair amount of precipitation just fine.

Gas brand signs, Osmond, NE

It was raining when I shot this row of gas station signs in Osmond from inside my dry car.

Sentinels of the Prairie, Jackson, NE

Plenty of clouds remained but rain was no longer falling by the time I reached the windmill farm near Jackson about an hour later. The windmills displayed at Sentinels of the Prairie are in the private collection of Leonard Gill who owns the landfill that they front. It's a free outdoor museum with many of the windmills described by large signs.

Less than half an hour after leaving the windmills I was entering Iowa where I almost immediately drove about two miles off route. The only member of the Corps of Discovery to die during the expedition is buried beside the Missouri River in Sioux City, and I've long wanted to visit his monument.

Charles Floyd Monument, Sioux City, IA

The Lewis and Clark expedition is remarkable for a number of reasons not the least of which that only one of its members died before it was completed. With raging rivers, steep mountain ranges, very large and strange animals, freezing winters, and unpredictable natives, there was plenty of opportunity. Sargent Charles Floyd, the corps' lone casualty, died of what is now believed to be a ruptured appendix. Assuming that is accurate, Floyd could just as easily have met the same fate while sitting at home as there was no known treatment for appendicitis at the time. That means that the Blackfoot warrior Lewis shot in the act of stealing horses is the only person to die *because* of the expedition. Though obviously unrelated, that shooting occurred the day after William Clark carved his name in Pompey's Pillar while the expedition was split into two groups.

After paying my respects to Sargent Floyd, I returned to Historic US 20 and departed Sioux City. There are a few places where the current and historic routes are one and the same for a few miles but they are largely distinct all across Iowa. Sometimes the current alignment is north of the older one, sometimes it's to the south, and I can't tell which side is the most popular without measuring and calculating. I suppose it is possible that there are wonderful things on the current US 20 that I missed by driving the historic route, but it's a fact that people sticking to the current Route 20 miss out on things like the two jet fighter planes parked in Correctionville and the World's Largest Popcorn Ball in Sac City.

World's Largest Popcorn Ball, Sac City, IA

Sac City was the first to claim the popcorn ball title back in 1995. Apparently the Sac City ball went through a couple remakes after the 1995 2,225 pounder and was holding the record at 5,060 pounds when Indiana came up with a 6,510 pound ball at the 2013 state fair. Even though the Indiana ball lasted only until the fair closed and it was fed to livestock, it very firmly grabbed Sac City's attention. Residents and businesses in the Iowa town rose to the challenge and constructed the current 9,370 pound champion in 2016.

Former US 20 (Zearing Ave), Somers, IA

Some of Historic US 20 in Iowa does remain unpaved but I believe I drove every bit of it, and every gravel section I drove was straight enough and smooth enough to be an airplane runway.

It was almost exactly one month ago, just a few days after my trip began, that I met Historic US Route 20 Association founder Bryan Farr at the visitor center in Massachusetts. Now, just a few days before the trip's end, we are meeting again. Back in Massachusetts, Bryan told me of his plans to be in Iowa sometime in July. As I approached the state, we started zeroing in on where our paths might cross.

A major Historic US 20 signing project had just been completed in Iowa and Bryan headed out to help celebrate. The main event, with state officials, was scheduled for Monday, July 12, in Fort Dodge. Bryan arrived in Iowa a few days early in order to thank various groups and individuals involved and to participate in some photo ops and other events. He would be meeting with some folks in Manchester on Friday, and I managed to join him with some minor schedule tweaks. Manchester is the county seat of Delaware County and the meeting site was the Delaware County Courthouse.

Historic US Route 20 Association photo op, Manchester, IA

One purpose of these meetings was to get some pictures for use in local promotions, and I got a picture too. That's Manchester's Mayor, Milt Kramer, standing next to Bryan. I did not get names for the others in the photo.

Of course, the most most basic reason for Bryan even being in Iowa, or for his creation of the association for that matter, was promotion of Historic US Route 20. That is exactly what he was doing, via an interview by a local radio station, when I left Manchester.

My remaining stops in Iowa were not directly related to the highway. Just beyond Dyersville, I slipped a few miles off of the planned route to make my second visit to the *Field of Dreams* movie site. The baseball diamond carved from a cornfield for the 1989 movie has become quite the tourist attraction. The place was being readied for its first ever Major League Baseball game, and there were several more structures on the site than when I first saw it in 2014. That game did take place on August 12 with the White Sox topping the Yankees 9 to 8.

In Dubuque, I went barely a block off route to ride the Fenelon Place Elevator.

Fenelon Place Elevator, Dubuque, IA

The original elevator was built to get one man, JK Graves, home for lunch. That was in 1882. JK's gardener operated the steam driven machinery that lowered his boss to work each morning brought him home and returned him after lunch and a nap, then brought him up one more time at the end of each workday. The whole thing has been much improved since then but, 120 years later, the machinery is still operated from the top.

Passengers heading up ring a bell when they are ready. Sometime later, the operator gives a warning with a buzzer before pulling the little car upward. All payments – cash only

– are made at the top. When Graves started charging his neighbors to ride his elevator, the fare was a nickle. Today it's two dollars each way but that seems like a fair price to ride what has been called "the world's steepest, shortest scenic railway".

The Mississippi River and a bridge to Illinois are less than a mile away from Fenelon Place and its famous funicular. The town of Gelena, where the U.S. Grant Home State Historic Site is located, is about a dozen miles beyond. There US 20 passes within a couple-hundred yards of Grant's Home. It takes noticeably more than 200 yards of driving to reach it, however.

Grant's Home, Galena, IL

Ulysses S. Grant was born in southern Ohio and I've visited his birthplace and childhood home multiple times. It always seemed strange to me that people consider Illinois to be his home and that he is buried in New York. I must admit, though, that this place is considerably more upscale than the tiny cabin he was born in or the modest brick house he grew up in. Apparently, that moving-on-up trend continued as I understand his tomb in New York City, which I've not seen, is the most impressive of the lot.

Fahrion Road near Woodbine, IL

Illinois does have some bypassed and unpaved stretches of former US 20 but they are few and well maintained.

Don Hatch, Perry Huntoon, Cort Stevens

As I neared Chicago and the eastern edge of Illinois, I had the unusual but very pleasant experience of meeting up with three friends in a row, in different places and at different times, with no real sightseeing in between. Rather than filling a page or two with pictures of friendly but not necessarily familiar faces, I've packaged the three meetings together. I met Don Hatch for a great hamburger at The Spot Tavern in Marengo – then met Perry Huntoon at Sew Hop'd Brewery in Huntley to wash it down. The next morning, after sleeping, showering, and changing shirts, I met Cort Stevens at Mozzafiato in Elgin for breakfast. The 'burger was less than half a block off the highway, the beer roughly five miles off, and breakfast was right on US 20.

Although I first met each of the three on road trips, passing through this cluster of friends could be seen as an indication that I was getting close to home. That was essentially true, and the fact that I was now in somewhat familiar territory made the appearance of heavy rain a lot more tolerable than it would have been almost anywhere else on the trip. There were points in the trip where the sort of rain I was now seeing would have been disastrous or at least altered the trip considerably.

Former Studebaker Proving Grounds, South Bend, IN

Several miles west of South Bend, Indiana, the current US 20 begins an arc to the north that enters the city from the northwest. The historic alignment continues due east to pass the former Studebaker Proving Grounds. The 840 acre site is marked by brick pillars that were once topped by glass globes. I got a snapshot of one through the wet windshield as I passed.

I thought of pushing on through to home from here but it was late enough in the day that I opted to spend one more night on the road. I spent it at a chain motel in South Bend with dinner at the former home of Clement Studebaker less than a quarter mile north of Historic US Route 20. It has operated as a restaurant (Tippecanoe Place) since 1980 and a brewery was added in 2018.

Amish gathering near Shipshewana, IN

Rain had naturally figured into my decision to stay in South Bend, and it paid off. I was able to photograph this large Amish gathering near Shipshewana in the dry. I imagine the attendees were possibly more happy than I that the rain had stopped. The pictured buggies are perhaps a third to a half of what was there. I'm fairly certain that this was the largest gathering of parked horses I've ever seen.

US 20 & US 127 intersection near Alverton, OH

I entered Ohio forty miles later, and was back where I started twenty miles after that. Yes, I did still have to drive home but this was where I had first headed east on Historic US Route 20 back on June 6.

11. Wrap

I had been on the road for thirty-seven days and, by the time I reached home, had driven 9,095 miles. As planned, the bulk of that was on the Historic US Route 20 and the Yellowstone Trail, both of which I essentially drove in their entirety. I say "essentially" because, while I probably omitted some miles unknowingly due to missed turns, wrong turns, or wrong information, there were miles I missed knowingly. In Washington, I knowingly omitted the miles of the southern Yellowstone Trail alignment through Walla Walla and, while I didn't exactly do it knowingly, I quickly became aware that I did not follow the proper route through Blewett Pass.

Roughly 240 of the miles driven were between my home and US 20, about 45 connected the target routes' eastern ends, and another 364 connected their western ends. The remaining 8,446 miles were spent driving the two historic highways in the book's title. My plotted Yellowstone Trail route was 3,494 miles and my plotted Historic US Route 20 route was 3,444 miles for a combined 6,938. That means I spent 1,508 miles getting food, gas, sleep, and lost..

The trip involved seventeen states. US 20 passes through twelve states; the Yellowstone Trail passed through thirteen. From Illinois east, both historic highways cross the same six states and often do it on the exact same path. West of Chicago, they are quite separate and share only Montana and Idaho. US 20 never enters Wisconsin, Minnesota, either of the Dakotas, or Washington. The Yellowstone Trail never entered Iowa, Nebraska, Wyoming, or Oregon.

Setting aside the north-south travel connecting my home to US 20, the entire trip had a latitude range of less than seven degrees. Since most of US 20 is well south of the Yellowstone Trail, I was surprised to see that the trip's northernmost and southernmost points were both on the YT. In Fort Wayne, Indiana, the YT dips below US 20's most southern point which is near Norwalk, Ohio. The trip's northernmost point is on the YT just west of Wilbur, Washington. For the sake of completeness, US 20's northernmost point is a little east of the Idaho-Montana border.

That seven degree range (actually 6.685°) translates to about 460 miles or much less than the distance from Tucson to Tucumcari. Despite being more than double the distance from Tahachapi to Tonopah, that's clearly not going to cover the climate differences seen on north-south routes like the Dixie or Jefferson Highways. However, due largely to that northwest heatwave, I did see temperatures range from the low 40s Fahrenheit to well above 110° F.

The USA's wide variations in other aspects were represented even better. I whined about the congestion in Boston but that was hardly the only place I passed through with high population density. Cleveland and Chicago immediately come to mind but there were plenty of others. At the other end of the scale were places like parts of Montana and Wyoming which seemed so remote that when I saw someone walking along the road my first thought was that they needed help. In between were numerous communities large enough to radiate a personality and make an impression but not so large that I couldn't pause to take a picture without getting honked at.

Road types also varied greatly. I mentioned alternating between 80 and 8 miles per hour in Montana depending on the road I was traveling. Montana and South Dakota were the only states on this trip where 80 MPH is sometimes legal but they were not the only states where a speed around 8 MPH was sometimes prudent. The roads traveled ranged from multi-lane expressways to narrow two-tracks with grass growing tall between the tracks. Surfaces ranged from nearly new asphalt and concrete to bare earth that had never seen a bit of hard pavement or even gravel. While Washington's Blewett Pass was the only place where, due to my own goof, I was on truly treacherous roadway, it was not the only place where considerable care was required and some risk was present.

I hesitate to mention the nearly rain-free weather I enjoyed because there is a bit of a dark side to it. Many of my dry miles were undoubtedly intertwined with the northwest's heatwave and the west coast's drought. It is a sad truth that one man's month of sunny driving is another man's five weeks of stifling heat and elevated forest-fire-risk.

Precipitation was present on only five of those thirty-seven days, and it mostly timed itself for minimal impact. The first rain was in eastern New York as I was following the Yellowstone Trail west on a road I had driven three days earlier while following US 20 east. The situation was the same when I entered Ohio in the rain two days later. The rain that came and went while I slept in Minnesota doesn't count. I was headed east in Yellowstone Park when I next encountered rain while driving. Some of it was fairly heavy and there is no doubt that it obscured some remarkable scenery, but my goal at the time was passing through the crowded park rather than taking in the sights.

I again hit drive-time rain just a few days later in Nebraska. This is the only time that I feel rain actually interfered with my enjoyment of new sights and such. I have since learned of a giant shamrock embedded in the streets of O'Neill, the official Irish capital of Nebraska, that I apparently drove over in the rain without even noticing. The fifth and final time I drove in rain was as I left Illinois for Indiana. This is an area that could possibly be considered my extended neighborhood as I am somewhat familiar with it and can reach it with relative ease. When the only thing rain is responsible for is missing one shamrock in nine-thousand miles and thirty-seven days, it can't really be considered a factor at all.

Of course people mean a lot more to a road trip than do miles, days, or degrees of either latitude or temperature. I got to reconnect with seven old friends and connect with four people in the real world that I'd previously known only on the telephone or internet. Plus I met several people like Teri and Howie, who I had no idea even existed before I left home, but, who made their parts of the road both enjoyable and memorable.

I take the "road" in road trip literally. No matter the size of the snack cache or the volume of the stereo, flying down an expressway in order to maximize time at some destination is not my idea of a road trip. For me, the *road* itself has to contribute something. I am not saying that expressways are bad things or that people who prefer them are wrong. I do what I enjoy and others should too.

Maybe the most important number for this trip isn't the number of miles driven or states visited. Maybe it's not even the number of friendships refreshed, enhanced, or initiated. Maybe the most important number for this trip is two.

Driving all of a historic highway often takes multiple outings although I have driven some from end to end in a single trip. Sometimes when I've done that, I have clocked some miles on other historic highways as well. But this book describes the first time I have driven the full length of two historic highways on one trip. Pairing the Yellowstone Trail and Historic US Route 20 allowed me to take a "round trip" crossing of the United States with no risk of boredom at any point.

Yes, two is definitely the most important number in this end-of-trip summary. Two is the number of historic highways driven end-to-end when driving just one of them would have been an excellent adventure. Driving Historic US Route 20 in 2021 and the Yellowstone Trail too was doubly excellent.

ABOUT THE AUTHOR

Denny Gibson is a retired software engineer living on the outskirts of Cincinnati, Ohio. He is addicted to driving two-lane highways and, since 1999, has documented his travels on them at DennyGibson.com. His photographs and writings have appeared in other travel books and magazines. His first travelogue was *By Mopar to the Golden Gate* which tells the story of driving the Lincoln Highway during its centennial year in a fifty year old car. This is his seventh.